Therapeutic Approaches in Work with Traumatized Children and Young People

Community, Culture and Change

(formerly Therapeutic Communities)

Series editors: Rex Haigh and Jan Lees

Community, Culture and Change encompasses a wide range of ideas and theoretical models related to communities and cultures as a whole, embracing key Therapeutic Community concepts such as collective responsibility, citizenship and empowerment, as well as multidisciplinary ways of working and the social origins of distress. The ways in which our social and therapeutic worlds are changing is illustrated by the innovative and creative work described in these books.

Asylum to Action
Paddington Day Hospital, Therapeutic Communities and Beyond
Helen Spandler
Therapeutic Communities 16
ISBN 978 1 84310 348 6

Dangerous and Severe – Process, Programme and Person
Grendon's Work
Mark Morris
Therapeutic Communities 15
ISBN 978 1 84310 226 7

The Time of Therapeutic Communities
People, Places and Events
Liam Clarke
Therapeutic Communities 12
ISBN 978 1 84310 128 4

Therapeutic Communities for Children and Young People
Edited by Adrian Ward, Kajetan Kasinski, Jane Pooley, Alan Worthington
Therapeutic Communities 10
ISBN 978 1 84310 096 6

Therapeutic Communities
Past, Present and Future
Edited by Penelope Campling and Rex Haigh
Foreword by John Cox
Therapeutic Communities 2
ISBN 978 1 85302 614 0

Introduction to Therapeutic Communities
David Kennard
Therapeutic Communities 1
ISBN 978 1 85302 603 4

Therapeutic Approaches in Work with Traumatized Children and Young People

Theory and Practice

Patrick Tomlinson

Foreword by Paul van Heeswyk

Community, Culture and Change 14

Jessica Kingley Publishers
London and Philadelphia

First published in 2004
by Jessica Kingsley Publishers
116 Pentonville Road
London N1 9JB, UK
and
400 Market Street, Suite 400
Philadelphia, PA 19106, USA

www.jkp.com

Printed digitally since 2009

Library of Congress Cataloging in Publication Data

Tomlinson, Patrick, 1962-
Therapeutic approaches in work with traumatized children and young people : theory and practice / Patrick Tomlinson ; Preface by Paul Van Heeswyk.-- 1st American pbk. ed.
p. cm. -- (Therapeutic communities ; 14)
Includes bibliographical references and index.
ISBN 1- 84985-312-6 (pbk.)
1. Psychic trauma in children--Treatment. I. Title. II. Series.
RJ506.P66T65 2004
618.92'8521--dc22

2003026800

British Library Cataloguing in Publication Data

A CIP catalogue record for this book is available from the British Library

ISBN 978 1 84985 312 5

Contents

Foreword

The developing self has fundamental needs that must be discerned by parents and carers. Infants begin their lives dependant on others to recognize and then realize their needs and wishes. Without this experience over time, they have little chance to become and know themselves. It is not, as Franklin Giddins once observed, that two heads are better than one. Rather, it is that two (or more) heads are needed for one. The infant is vulnerable to both a lack of empathic response from his carers and to intrusive assault, especially where adults use the infant as a receptacle for their own excesses or unmet needs. In the absence of empathic response to the infant's communications, emotional and psychological growth in the child is severely endangered.

The chapters in this book represent the empathic immersing of many therapeutic workers in the recorded experiences of a community of children who had suffered deprivation and abuse during the early months and years of their lives. This weekly group reflection sought to support the children's 24-hour care, the therapeutic aim of which was to set free and revitalize atrophied maturational processes in order that development could continue.

Maturational processes, of course, do not unfold solely and inevitably within the child but presuppose relationships. It is essential therefore to remember that the difficult or challenging behaviour of children is adaptive to the relationships into which they were born. Where a crying child meets, over time, no concerned response from his carer, or receives, instead, physical abuse, he will not recognise and feel his own sadness or pain. Emerging feeling states will constitute a source of danger and will need to be ignored or attacked, as they were by his carers.

Professionals refer sometimes, by way of shorthand, to 'unintegrated children', or to those with 'attachment disorders'. In such understandable attempts to give order to an otherwise bewildering presenting sequence of challenging behaviours, our language can in fact create new problems. We may speak as if the child's difficulties reside only within him. This becomes more than a linguistic issue when it begins to have implications for our capacity to remain hopeful about change or to maintain confidence in our own ability to be of value. At worst, we may commit ourselves, almost, to a vain search for modern variants of (and experts in) suppression or exorcism of the devil within. Trauma, for many, is a fact of life. But in the right kind of human environment, so too is recovery.

All parents know, however, that children need a different kind of relationship to their carers at each different stage of their lives to sustain growth. The parent of a baby relates in ways that will no longer be appropriate to the five-year-old child or to the adolescent. The challenge is always to reflect (preferably with sympathetic others) on the feelings and thoughts that come to us in response to the behavioural and verbal communications of the young people in our families, educational and therapeutic settings. Where sequences of behaviour or communications of feelings appear stuck and repetitive, or otherwise give cause for concern, it may be worth thinking what kind of change within the total relationship between child and carer may facilitate or release again a freer and more flexible movement and progress. On many occasions, this change may require only a shift in attitude or a small alteration of behaviour on the part of the adult. After all, when a parent complains about his child's symptoms, he may also be saying he does not feel competent, alone, to deal with the underlying problem (perhaps because it stimulates memories of his own difficulties as a child in his family of origin). Where this can be acknowledged to be the case, the observations of partners, extended family, friends or colleagues are an important resource.

The ideas expressed in this book are the outcome of exactly this kind of resource in action. Indeed, the weekly discussions of this selection of themes took place in the meetings of the Cotswold Community Therapeutic Resource Group, where workers took time to reflect on the emotional turmoil of life with troubled children. I, myself, would welcome the day when parents can form themselves into versions of this type of support group within their own local communities, to think together about the issues that arise in the day-to-day care of their children. I am anyway certain that the thoughts and observations contained in these attempts at understanding the sometimes hazardous psychological birth and development of the human infant within relationship to important others will prove stimulating and helpful to all those who care for and work with children.

It was the belief of Donald Winnicott and Barbara Dockar-Drysdale, whose work inspired that of the Cotswold Community, that the meeting of certain basic emotional and physical needs by carers within the infant's first year of life is a developmental imperative. Babies need to be fed when hungry, clothed and cleaned, and held safely through the moments of their distress. They need to be celebrated and to participate in delighted exchanges. They need also to be protected from dangerous intrusions and impingements. This kind of care is of course the regular and inevitable consequence of parental love within all cultures. Without these early levels of active response and protection, the child's emotional life may remain frozen and her development come to a standstill, despite the appearance of growth.

However, for the slightly older child, failures in being understood, when within the context of genuine efforts at empathy, may be upsetting for all concerned yet constitute, nevertheless, a necessary and even optimal frustration. Honest parental mistakes stimulate the child to progress, inside the safety of the caring relationship, towards increasing levels of independence. This wise and compassionate Winnicottian view informs the principles within this book. Some things in the care of our children we simply cannot afford to get wrong. But in many other respects, our best attempts at shared empathic thinking are more than good enough.

Paul van Heeswyk
Association of Child Psychotherapists

Acknowledgements

This book is based upon the work of a staff group at the Cotswold Community from 1994–2000. I would like to thank and acknowledge the following people.

The senior therapeutic practitioners who were members of the group at different times. The following people contributed thoughts, questions, principles and therapeutic approaches that are described in this book:

Jennifer Browner, Liz Buffham, Angus Burnett, Nicky Dillon Sean Dunne, Jim Hamil, Stuart Hannah, Vanessa Haughey, Susan Holroyd, Debbie Hopper, Jill Huntley, Niall Kelly, Stephen Lund, Shelagh Molloy, Lillian Morris, Theresa Salter and Jaana Virtanen.

John Whitwell who was the principal throughout the period this work is based upon. Peter Millar, Pat Hancock, Kay Malko and Chris Knight who were the senior management team during this time. Through effective leadership and management, this team provided the necessary conditions in which therapeutic work could take place.

Mark Thomas, a colleague whom I worked with at the community, for his enthusiasm and for planting the idea of publication.

I would like to acknowledge the legacy of Barbara Dockar-Drysdale who was consultant child psychotherapist to the Community for 20 years, and who established the work of the group described in this book. Paul van Heeswyk followed Dockar-Drysdale in this role and was consultant to the group throughout the six-year period this book is based upon. I would like to thank him for his ability to be receptive, thoughtful and optimistic.

Dave Forrest, Director of Children's Services, NCH–South West Region, who has supported the publication of this book and the use of material that derived from the Community.

Mary Walsh and Andrew Constable, chief executive and managing director of SACCS, my employer. SACCS has supported the work that has been necessary to develop and edit the book. Terry Philpot who has given thoughtful advice on the text, improving its clarity.

Finally, but not least, I would like to thank my wife Georgia for her support, our children Patsy and Daniel, and my parents June and Don – 'Home is where we start from.' (Winnicott 1986)

Introduction

'Trauma' can be understood to mean a profound emotional shock (Oxford Dictionary 1992). The theme of this book is thinking about children in a way that may help them to recover from their emotional traumas. Often, profound trauma in early childhood affects the whole of the child's development, causing serious delays and distortions. In some cases, the child's physical health and growth can suffer. For normal development to be recovered, the trauma needs to be understood. If a child is fortunate, this understanding can happen spontaneously at the time of the trauma. Such an understanding occurring may prevent long-term damage, for example, a grandparent who is emotionally attuned and empathetic where a child is traumatized within the immediate family. This support might just make the trauma comprehensible to the child so that the experience can be endured, thought about and integrated. Without some kind of supportive emotional involvement, the trauma remains as an unthinkable experience that continues to haunt the child (Fraiberg 1980). The child may experience this as a nameless dread (Copley and Forryan 1987, p.246) and be consumed by it, so that further emotional development is put on hold. Another possibility is that the child cuts off emotionally and seems emotionally frozen (Dockar-Drysdale 1958), feeling nothing real. The child who is highly anxious and the child who is emotionally frozen are both lacking the capacity to form attachments, receive nourishment, and engage in the ordinary experiences that enable growth and development. Referring to a child who was severely traumatized during the first year and who would chew cactus leaves, Bettleheim (1990) describes another possible reaction to trauma:

> By inflicting on himself a parallel pain, he tried not only to obliterate through pain the mental images which tortured him, but to convince himself that he could be in control of a pain over which he had been able to

> exercise no control whatsoever, when it had destroyed him as a human being. (p.35)

Trauma is an experience that potentially can be recovered from and even made use of. An experience that cannot be made use of is one that threatens to damage a person permanently. The extent to which a trauma can be thought about and integrated within the person's experience will depend upon a number of factors, such as the emotional resources available to the person during the trauma and the nature of the trauma. The emotional resources include those of the individual experiencing the trauma and the support provided by others. The nature of the trauma includes the severity of the traumatic experience and the frequency of the experience.

A traumatized child needs to make sense of the trauma so that it can be put into perspective. The shock of the trauma can cause a regression in the child's development. A person who is in shock cannot think or attend to ordinary things. Regression can be a defensive falling back to trigger a supportive and protective response from others. This aspect of trauma leads to the need for both understanding and nurture. The nurture is necessary to fill the gap in development that has been created and to establish a sense of security that makes it feel safe to move forwards again.

To some extent, every child experiences traumas or shocks to their sense of being. Most of the time, these shocks are recognized by a carer and responded to, so the child quickly returns to a sense of continuity. Even if the shocks are not noticed, they may not dominate the child's experience. The child learns that shocks can be recovered from and are not overwhelming. The shock that can be thought about can provide experience and knowledge of some of life's difficulties. This enables a child to anticipate difficulties and develop positive ways of managing them. It is hard to imagine how we would otherwise have any capacity to cope with the major shocks experienced throughout life. In this sense, child development can be seen to include the experience of trauma and the recovery from trauma. The recovery from trauma is a healing process that can be called therapeutic. The theme of this book is relevant to all people involved in the development of children, whether in a parental, educational, caring or therapeutic role. However, this book is focused on therapeutic work with children who have suffered an extreme and specific type of trauma.

These children have suffered persistent and multiple trauma in the first years of life, where their own emotional resources were very limited. At the same time, they have received little or no emotional containment from their parents and family. In some cases, the child's whole environment could be described as constantly traumatic. These children had suffered such significant emotional disturbance that they had not developed emotionally, beyond the state of unintegration normally associated with an infant during the first year of life (Winnicott 1962).

There is not a simple solution to trauma and recovery. Recovery from trauma cannot be prescribed, but needs an environment where it is safe to think about the trauma, experience feelings about it and make reliable provision to heal the trauma. This type of environment has been referred to as a 'holding environment' (Miller 1993; Ward 1998). Healing deep-rooted trauma is a demanding task. Severely traumatized children have often become extremely antisocial, highly defended and developmentally delayed. They may be compulsively and repeatedly preoccupied in trying to do everything possible to keep the trauma out of consciousness. They could be constantly preoccupied by trauma, but in a way that offers no relief or resolution. They might have no conscious ability to think about the trauma, but continually reenact the trauma in an attempt to somehow make sense of it or evoke an understanding response from others. They may be desperately trying to forget the trauma and take flight from their feelings. Attempts to make steps forwards and towards others will constantly be disrupted by fears and anxieties.

Children who have suffered trauma in the earliest years and who have endured many further years of being misunderstood and let down, will not readily allow themselves to be helped. Allowing trust to develop is very threatening. These children are likely to attack the efforts of those trying to help them. If thinking about the children is part of the help, we can expect the thinking to be rejected and attacked (Copley and Forryan 1987, p.258). Creating an environment where it is possible to think about the children and their experiences is critical to their recovery. There is not always a right or wrong answer in work with traumatized children any more than there is to every difficulty arising in childhood. There are signposts and reference points but each child and each situation is unique. Children need to be cared for by people who have emotional strength and experience to draw upon, enough useful signposts and reference points, but also the capacity to think about each situation and child as unique. Therefore developing a way of thinking about children is most important.

Writing about his experience as a leader of a therapeutic community for children and referring to a talk given by Dockar-Drysdale, Rollinson (2003) describes the importance of thinking and being able to tolerate uncertainty:

> She spoke to them about the dangers of becoming complacent or certain. She declared that the work must always proceed in a way that can tolerate doubt or not knowing. Only in this way can we hope to ensure that we are carrying on thinking. It is in absolutist or crisis cultures that there is no doubt; there is only absolute certainty. A culture with structures, bound-

> aries and spaces will support thought. Thought will contain uncertainty and, thus, thoughtful responses can be made to the children, not only when adults are supporting healthy functioning but even when they are managing breakdown. The emotional 'mess' can be tolerated, and dealing with it can remain at the core of our work. It need not be driven out. Of course the sufferings of uncertainty are real, but nothing like the eventual suffering born of absolute certainty. (p.218)

He goes on to state the 'true nature of our work' with traumatized children:

> Our focus should be less upon getting answers for someone and more about identifying (and helping the person to identify) the value that lies deep within each child, a child who almost always feels entirely worthless and unwantable on joining us. (p.219)

Emotional unintegration and integration

Throughout the book the terms 'unintegrated' and 'integrated' will be used to describe a child's stage of development. 'Unintegrated' is the term Winnicott (1962) used to describe the emotional state of the infant from birth and during the first few months of life. Winnicott ascertained that the 'holding' of the infant by the mother enables the infant to mature towards integration. He describes how 'holding' gives the infant an experience of being gathered together, which makes him a unit self – a whole person living in the body. At these moments the fragments of the unintegrated infant are held together creating a sense of integration. This process is gradually internalized by the infant enabling him to build an expectation of his needs being met. He also gradually internalizes the mother's capacity to organize and hold his world together, enabling him to do this for himself. If the infant is protected from impingement (Dockar-Drysdale 1960b), he is able to face external reality from a sense of security and of his existence as a person in that world. Winnicott describes the infant moving from unintegration to integration normally by the end of the first year. The integrated infant is a person in his own right, consciously aware of his separateness from his mother and of his dependence on her. He has a clear sense of self and is able to manage some of his anxieties. However, during the initial stages of integration the infant has to cope with anxiety caused by awareness of his separation and dependence. The infant at this stage also has a fear of disintegration and losing the newly achieved capacities associated with emotional integration (Dockar-Drysdale 1990a). Children who have serious disruptions to provision during the first year are likely to remain unintegrated until they are provided with the necessary experiences of primary provision. Dockar-Drysdale (1990a) states:

> Those who are deprived and who have failed to integrate regress in the course of treatment to *the point of failure* (Winnicott). This may be at any stage of development. Children *know* the point to which they need to return, just as they *know* what they need as symbolic adaptations.
>
> The failure (of maternal provision) will be in the course of the first years and is fixed like a fly in amber in the unconscious memory. (p.42)

Children who fail to achieve emotional integration due to trauma and deprivation can be described as children who are suffering from attachment disorder. In particular, they could be described as suffering from disorganized attachment disorder. Fonagy (2001) argues that, 'Winnicott's theory is traditionally regarded as compatible with attachment theory formulations' (p.102). Referring to disorganized attachment he also states, 'The disorganized pattern could be reformulated as an indication of the relative immaturity of the ego and its inability to muster coherent strategies of response' (p.69), and 'As we have seen, disorganized attachment is principally a set of rather contradictory and certainly unintegrated behaviour strategies' (p.136). Referring to the work of Karlen Lyons-Ruth, Fonagy explains how a disorganized attachment can be caused by both a severe trauma to an adequately attached child and the primary caregiver's failure over time to provide optimal attachment opportunities. Most of the children at the Cotswold Community had suffered both of these experiences.

Emotional containment

Many solutions to children's difficulties come from the kind of thought provided by carers that is partly conscious and partly unconscious. This process has been described as 'emotional containment' (Bion 1962). Bion developed the concept of a 'container' into which feelings are projected. This is an activity shared by two individuals and is a predominant aspect of the mother-infant relationship. The infant's fears and anxieties are projected into the maternal container. The mother is able to hold onto these feelings, think about them consciously and unconsciously, and then return the feelings back to the infant, but in a more tolerable form. The infant also takes in and internalizes the feeling of being contained. He experiences his mother's emotional availability and capacity to bear and think about his anxieties. Gradually through this experience, the infant develops his own capacity for emotional containment.

The concept of containment is central to work with traumatized children and will be referred to throughout this book. The thinking environment needs to be strong and resilient if it is going to survive. This book gives an example of how such an environment was established and enabled many traumatized children to recover. These children were often at 'the end of the road' and without help would end up with a hopeless life, possibly causing severe damage to others as well as themselves. The help provided enabled many of them to overcome trauma and live a constructive life.

The book draws its experience from the Cotswold Community, which was established as a residential therapeutic community in the late 1960s to provide treatment for emotionally disturbed boys and continues to do so. From the beginning, the Community knew the children had suffered traumas that had seriously delayed and distorted their capacity to think and make attachments. A strong culture was created, where thinking and attachments were central to the work. Staff had regular team meetings, supervision, consultancy and training. The approach encouraged staff to try continually to understand the meaning of their experiences at work. All behavior of children and staff was believed to have meaning. If meaning could be found there would be the opportunity of learning, growth and letting go of the past. Staff provided a highly nurturing environment and the opportunity for reliable relationships, which could meet the emotional dependency needs of the children.

The basis of this book comes from the work of a staff group that met weekly to discuss therapeutic issues, with the aim of developing understanding and relating theory to practice. The Community found the process of thinking about children, their difficulties and needs helpful to the children's recovery. The book first aims to show what can be gained from establishing such a process. Second, the aim is to discuss specific matters involved in the work and to give some practical guidance as well as to encourage thinking about the subject. When individual cases are being thought about it can help to start with a range of possibilities of what may be happening. This can help us to decide the most appropriate way of working. The subjects covered are by no means exhaustive and are not meant to provide a comprehensive approach.

An approach to therapeutic work with children must first of all aim to develop a way of doing things and thinking. The matters and dynamics that will arise in this work are infinite. If those working with children can experience what seems incomprehensible, stick with it and make sense of it, it may be possible for children to feel we can help them do the same.

The style of the book aims to reflect discussions that took place on each subject. In most cases, the content under a heading will have been the subject of a one-hour group discussion. The work from the discussions would be shared widely within the Community, partly to give direction to the therapeutic task and to generate further thought and discussion. As the book is written from work evolving it provides a historical record of work in a therapeutic community in a way that combines theoretical matters with the reality of day-to-day life and work.

Each chapter covers a significant aspect of therapeutic work with traumatized children and begins with a summary of the theme. Each subject within the chapter begins with an explanation of the context. For the sake of economy, the male gender will be used in reference to the child and female for the staff. The word 'adult' or 'grown-up' will be used in relation to staff. Dockar-Drysdale (1969) often explained that 'grown-up' gave a sense of a person evolving:

> I very rarely use the word 'adult', preferring to say 'grown-up'. Adult seems to deny that *a child has grown up*, confirming the split which many parents and children feel divides them from each other. (p.27)

Grown-up asks the question, grown-up from what? The answer is from a child. This can help bridge the gap for a child who sees an adult as far removed with no connection to his own experience.

Chapter 1

The Cotswold Community

The Cotswold Community was created as a residential therapeutic community in 1967 to provide treatment for emotionally disturbed and deprived boys. The boys lived in a number of separate houses in a village-type setting on a 350-acre farm. Education was provided on site. Social services, education and health departments referred boys from all over Britain. All of the boys had experienced severe deprivation, disruption and trauma in infancy as well as later childhood and were assessed as emotionally unintegrated.

Normally boys were admitted between the ages of 8 and 13 before the onset of adolescence. On admission, the boys joined one of three primary houses (for explanation of primary and secondary houses see below). The treatment took place within the integrated living and education environment. Every part of the Community was linked and the design of its management structure reflected the treatment task.

As a boy evolved and reached emotional integration, he either left the Community from the primary house or was referred to the secondary house for a further stage of treatment and consolidation. All of the houses had places for ten boys.

The Community's therapeutic approach was largely based upon Barbara Dockar-Drysdale's application of Donald Winnicott's psychoanalytic theory of child development and treatment (Dockar-Drysdale 1990a, 1993a). Winnicott's ideas are particularly relevant to work with children who have been traumatized during infancy. Approaches derived from the work of psychoanalysts Melanie Klein and Wilfred Bion among others were also incorporated. The organizational and management structure was based on an open systems model developed through close work with consultants from the Tavistock Institute of Human Relations. This consultancy spanned a 30-year period, beginning with A.K. Rice, who was followed by Isobel Menzies Lyth and then Eric Miller. Careful attention was paid to ensure that the structure adopted and all aspects of the Community were supportive of the treatment task.

The staff group consisted of residential social workers (care staff), teachers, domestic staff, maintenance staff, administration staff, farm workers, volunteers and students. A senior management team was responsible for the running of the Community as a whole. All of the residential social workers and teachers lived on site. These staff worked 65 or more hours a week to provide a high level of consistency and continuity for the boys.

After being admitted to a house a boy was assigned one of the residential social workers as a focal-carer. This relationship then became a focus for a boy's treatment. Normally a boy developed a dependant relationship with his carer and was able to receive primary provision (Dockar-Drysdale 1966, 1990a) that helped to fill the emotional gaps resulting from early deprivation. Each boy would also have a regular twice-weekly meeting with another member of the staff team. This meeting provided another reliable and protected space in which therapeutic communication could take place.

In the early years, each boy's education would aim to develop his educational abilities in a broad sense as well as to provide continuity in meeting his emotional needs. The education areas (rooms or classes) for emotionally unintegrated boys were called 'polys' (polytechnics) and the area for the more integrated boys called 'the small school'. The use of these names was partly to reflect the broad nature of the education but also to distinguish it from school, from which many of the boys were alienated. In recent years, there has been a concern to ensure that looked-after children and young people are not excluded from education. The word 'school' has been used to make the link with mainstream education.

Following the initial period when the Cotswold Community was overseen by the Home Office, Wiltshire County Council became the governing body until it was acquired by NCH in 1997. Following the acquisition by NCH the Community's registration changed from that of children's home with education to a school.

The therapeutic resource role

Each house team of six residential social workers had its own manager who then delegated specific areas of responsibility to the staff team. These covered responsibilities such as food and domestic matters, culture and play, therapeutic provision and administration. The team member responsible for the area of therapeutic provision was called a 'therapeutic resource'. The responsibility of this role focused on the treatment of each individual child as well as the therapeutic environment for the group as a whole. To help achieve these aims the therapeutic resource provided supervision for each of the residential social workers who had key relationships with individual children. They also worked with and supported the team as a whole on matters of treatment. This role acted as a 'therapeutic conscience' within the team, ensuring that therapeutic matters remained in the picture alongside more predominantly managerial ones. Communication between individual team members and within the whole team was central to the treatment task. To aid this process further, each team had a weekly consultancy with the consultant child psychotherapist.

The therapeutic resource worked closely with teachers so that care and education aspects of a child's treatment were integrated together appropriately. This allowed a shared understanding of how both contributed to a child's development. Eventually, this also led to the development of a therapeutic resource role within the education team to ensure that the development of the education task was linked to the wider context of the therapeutic approach and vice versa.

The therapeutic resources had regular individual consultancies with the child psychotherapist, as well as supervision with a senior manager on treatment matters.

The therapeutic resource meeting

This was a weekly one-hour meeting, where the therapeutic resources met as a group with the consultant child psychotherapist. Dockar-Drysdale initially established this meeting and was consultant to the group until 1990. Paul van Heeswyk followed in the role of consultant child psychotherapist. The role of the consultant was to provide an external perspective and to help staff think about their work, to help develop their understanding and awareness. Between 1994 and 2000 the task of the meeting was defined as 'constantly to review our therapeutic practice with the aim of ensuring its optimal development'.

The meeting provided a space for thinking things through together outside of the immediate workplace. The meeting continually reviewed all areas of work examining the link between theory and practice. The existence of the meeting in itself acted as a container for anxieties related to treatment, enabling people to understand their work more effectively outside of the meeting. The meeting produced feedback to the whole staff group, keeping issues alive. The aim was to conceptualize matters arising and link theory to practice. This book is based upon discussions that took place in meetings between 1994 and 2000. Subjects have been grouped into sections under different themes. Throughout this period chair of the meetings was Patrick Tomlinson (Assistant Principal – Cotswold Community).

Chapter 2

Primary Provision – Theory and Practice

It is usual for a child's primary carers, most commonly his parents, to provide for him. This is highly personal and intimate and the carer will be sensitized and attuned to the infant's needs. The most important part of this provision is the carer's own emotional involvement, which will evolve around the physical and emotional needs of the infant. We call this type of care 'nurturing'. It consists of love and emotional warmth, closeness and intimacy, all of which give the infant a feeling of being loved and wanted. This contributes to the infant's sense of emotional security and its ability to attach to others. Winnicott (1956a) referred to the emotional condition of the carer in such a situation as 'primary maternal preoccupation'.

However, the primary provision of many traumatized children has often been interrupted or inadequate, which leaves gaps in their experience and emotional development. The infant will continue to need primary provision until these gaps are filled. Primary provision lays the foundations for development and without such provision development will be disturbed. It is, therefore, essential that in our work with traumatized children we identify and meet the child's need for primary provision.

Adaptation to need (the provision of 'special things')

The provision of 'adaptations' became central to the therapeutic approach (Dockar-Drysdale 1961). Adaptations can be provided in any setting where a child has the need for primary provision because of early childhood trauma and deprivation. The provision of adaptations was always carefully assessed and discussions would take place between the staff team and consultant before a provision could be made.

During infancy, a baby needs a high level of adaptation. When a baby is highly dependant, the world around him adapts to meet his needs. He is not yet ready to be frustrated and his reaching out is met by a preoccupied grown-up. The adaptation helps maintain the baby's illusion of being in control and omnipotent. A mother will respond in all manner of ways to her infant which are unique to their relationship. For example, an infant may like to be held and rocked in a certain way, while a specific lullaby is sung to him. This will have developed in an intuitive way and once established the mother will know how to respond to the infant at a given moment. The routine may also become a pattern at certain times of the day. It is the emotional involvement of the mother with her infant that makes the provision particularly meaningful and enjoyable to the infant.

The children we work with have not experienced 'good enough' adaptation to their needs during infancy. Adaptations are a way of responding to the need for regression. Regression can be the search for missing relationship experiences, the need in the present to have a developmental experience that has been missed in the past. An adaptation symbolically represents the quality of provision and relationship the child has missed.

Adaptations normally develop within the context of a specific relationship where a child is beginning to trust a grown-up and feel attached. As the relationship between a child and preoccupied grown-up develops, a gesture may come from the child, indicating how his needs can be met. When this happens we should let the child know we are aware of his need and will think carefully about it. It is not necessary to ask him why he desires something, the relevant thing is how the adaptation is reached, the meaning it has for the child and grown-up, and how it is provided. The provision can be seen as symbolic rather than an attempt to provide a child with what he has actually missed. For example, a child having a special story and drink, twice a week, reliably with the same grown-up, protected from disruption. The child may feel particularly excited about these times, and may feel and appear much younger than he is. For example, a 12-year-old using a teddy and talking in a babyish voice, though at other times he relates to the grown-up in more of an age-appropriate way. Though we may feel this is close to the actual provision he missed, it may represent an even earlier experience such as being held by his mother and fed. If the adaptation has clear boundaries around it, the child may be able to make positive use of it and distinguish between this 'special time' and other times. If it works in this way it is possible that the need to regress can be localized around the adaptation.

A localized regression means that the need to regress is focused within a specific relationship, within a certain time and with clear boundaries in terms of what is provided. If this is provided reliably the child is more able at other times to function at an age-appropriate level knowing he has this special provision (Dockar-Drysdale 1963b).

Adaptations can be food, but can also be provided in other ways. For example, a child might ask a grown-up to provide a special food, while another might want to do a special activity together. It is likely that the child will find something that can be provided by the grown-up in a way that is meaningful and satisfying to both of them. It is important, however, to be sure that it is meeting the child's need and he is not 'trying to please' the grown-up in a false way (Winnicott 1960a). Some children are worried about doing things to please the grown-up.

As the child takes in this experience and stores it emotionally, his need for the adaptation will gradually diminish. This is similar to the process of weaning. Any changes in the provision during this time need to be thought about carefully and will probably reflect a child moving through to emotional maturity. An adaptation specifically emerges out of a dependant attachment and before emotional integration is reached.

The grown-up should discuss this provision in supervision and consultancy. If the adaptation is to be provided, the whole team should know about it, so that the provision can be supported and protected. It must be provided reliably. Once the provision of adaptations has developed, they will become a significant part of the house culture and issues will arise around them, of which the following questions are examples:

- How should we respond to a child who is asking for a baby's bottle?
- Could two children in the same house be provided with the same adaptation?
- Can a food adaptation be something 'out of a packet' rather than something made by the grown-up?

The adaptation has an 'as if' quality to it and if it becomes too close to the actual thing, it loses this quality and becomes more like an actual substitute. A baby's bottle feels too close to the actual provision for a baby to maintain an 'as if' quality. It could feel that we are trying to provide a substitute experience. If this were the case, it would not be a useful provision. It would be difficult for the provision to remain localized as it may feel that we were offering the child an opportunity to really be a baby. We need to hold onto the reality that we cannot actually provide this experience.

During a child's treatment, we will need to work with him on the losses experienced in early childhood. By providing an adaptation that is representative of early primary provision rather than a concrete substitute for it, we enable a child to use the provision meaningfully and hold onto the reality of his past experiences. We also maintain a clear boundary between a child's experiences as an infant and in the here and now, and our roles as carers rather than as parents. These boundaries can easily become confused for emotionally unintegrated children so we need to be clear about them.

If a child asks for a baby's bottle and it seems he really wants something he can suck a drink out of, it should be possible to find something similar, but which is also different. We should keep in mind that it is not the actual thing being provided that is most significant but the relationship within which it is provided. If there is too much focus on the special thing itself, this could be a displacement of feelings and anxieties about the relationship. A defining aspect of the adaptation is that it is special between the individual child and grown-up. The nature of the relationship is special and the special thing is representative of this. To help maintain this sense of 'specialness' we encourage some privacy around adaptations. A grown-up would not tell a child about another child's adaptation. We would explain that it is special and private, between the individual child and grown-up. Saying that something is private is not the same as being secretive. Sometimes children talk about their special things with each other and spoil the provision by rejecting or dismissing it. If two children are having the same thing, this could undermine the sense of 'specialness' for the children and grown-ups involved. If two grown-ups are providing the same thing, there is also the danger that the grown-ups begin to look upon the special things as interchangeable. Whether two children could be provided with the same adaptation will depend upon the staff team being able to maintain the culture around special things, without the provision for an individual child being diminished.

There are similar questions in relation to whether the special thing is made by the grown-up or bought pre-made. It is necessary that the special thing has a quality that feels personal to the child and grown-up. If the grown-up makes the special thing, this requires some personal investment, as does buying it and ensuring that it is provided reliably. However, the way it is given to the child from the grown-up is what matters most. Adaptations are difficult to provide reliably over time. There will at times be ambivalence for the grown-up and child about giving and receiving special things. There will also be feelings towards the child and grown-up involved from other grown-ups and children. Because of this difficulty and their importance, special things are supported and protected by the structure around them.

The whole team always knows when one is being provided and the grown-up involved is never asked to do anything else at those times. It may be necessary to have other conditions in the areas discussed above to create a culture that is resistant to a tendency towards impersonal provision.

Working with omnipotent behavior

According to the Oxford Dictionary (1992) 'omnipotent' means having absolute power and was often used, usually by staff referring to a child who was exasperatingly demanding. Therefore, the word could take on negative connotations portraying omnipotence in a pathological way.

However, omnipotence is also an essential developmental experience (Winnicott 1960a, pp.145–146). In a 'good enough' environment, a baby's illusion of omnipotence is met and protected, allowing him to maintain this illusion. This illusion makes his absolute state of dependency tolerable for him. Through this experience, the baby is gradually able to build up the internal resources that enable him to experience frustration and for his omnipotence to be challenged. The baby begins to realize that he is not in control of all around him. The children we work with have experienced this loss of control before they were ready. Too early, they have been coerced into an awareness of others' needs and into feeling powerless and impotent. This leads to a great sense of mistrust and anger at being let down, so the omnipotence of children here is often tinged with this anger and mistrust. This makes working with the omnipotence more difficult.

In a 'good enough' environment, the mother who can allow her baby to use her may also enjoy a baby's omnipotence. To work with and at times enjoy the children's omnipotence we need to let ourselves be used by them. The idea of being used is central to our work and how we respond to omnipotence. If we acknowledge this as a need, we will need to acknowledge our own experiences of omnipotence and any envy we feel towards the child. He has something we once had and partly wish we could still have.

It is possible to be on the side of the omnipotent wish without actually meeting it. Needs must be met but wishes and desires may be frustrated. If we can recognize a child's need for omnipotence, we may feel compassionate about his attempts to control us. The extent to which a child's omnipotence is met and the extent to which he is able to face external reality will depend on his developmental needs, as he moves from emotional unintegration to integration.

Emotional preoccupation and the provision we make for children

The specific positive quality of the staff's work was often summarized as being preoccupied with the children. This was regarded as a positive emotional and professional state of mind and was derived from Winnicott's (1956a) description of a mother's primary maternal preoccupation with her infant. As with motherhood, this state of mind could be idealized and not being preoccupied could become the equivalent of not being a 'good enough' mother. We attempted to discuss this concept and understand the emotional content of our views on staff's level of preoccupation.

Primary maternal preoccupation refers to the highly attuned state of the mother in relation to her infant, just before and after birth. At times our work involves levels of preoccupation that have some similarity with this, while also being different.

We use the idea of preoccupation in different ways:

- to describe what a child needs in terms of primary provision;
- to describe an adult who is preoccupied with a child in a positive way;
- to describe an adult who is preoccupied, but with other things rather than work and is distracted.

On occasions, an adult is told in a judgmental way that she is not preoccupied. The issue of preoccupation needs thinking about carefully. If it is perceived that an adult is not preoccupied, a number of things need considering:

- Maybe the adult is worried or upset about something external and needs support with that.
- The adult could be cutting off emotionally or using other defenses, to protect herself from being overwhelmed by threatening or painful feelings. A safe environment is necessary if these defenses are to be let go.
- The child may need the adult not to be preoccupied or thinking about him. The child could need space, to have an experience of separation. Over-preoccupation can be as problematic as a lack of it. For example, an adult could be thinking all of a child's thoughts for him, and always knowing what a child needs before he knows himself.

- Children we work with can feel threatened by preoccupation and being thought about. Although a child may need preoccupation, his sense of vulnerability and dependence will also be heightened, which can be quite frightening. Our preoccupation or thinking may be constantly attacked, or turned into something else by the child, such as intrusion or abuse.
- Whatever we are or are not thinking and feeling when we are with a child, might tell us something about him and our relationship with him. For instance, if we find we are forgetting things for a certain child, what may this tell us? We do not care enough? The child is afraid of being forgotten or wants to be forgotten? The child wants to forget something? He feels he is not worth remembering?
- Our thoughts that other people are not preoccupied could be a projection of a fear we have about ourselves. We may have a fear of becoming the non-listening, non-caring, non-attentive parent.

What kind of thinking and attentiveness are we trying to provide for children? It is necessary that we are very attentive to a child's communication and needs, and our own thoughts and feelings. To achieve this receptive state of mind we need to try to make sense of our own thoughts and feelings, in terms of what is connected to what. We should use and be attentive to each other in this process, discussing with each other what we think is going on. This helps to provide feedback that we can use to test and evaluate our own feelings and opinions. Sometimes it might not be possible to think about a child, or even to notice one is not doing this. Again, we should help each other with this. Mostly, feelings or thoughts of not being bothered, interested or concerned are only unproductive if they are not acknowledged or listened to appropriately.

If a child is having a difficult time, often a carer can feel guilty that it is her fault, and this is reinforced by comments by other staff such as ‘where is your preoccupation?’. It is supportive to try to get alongside each other and try to help the child through this time. His difficulties could even be related to a sense of being thought about or cared for. The idea that good work always means feeling or being preoccupied can be felt as an impossible burden, which is counter-productive to being receptive, thoughtful and responsive to a child's needs.

Transitional objects and the use of teddy bears

Teddies were an important part of the culture and were used by the children in different ways. The ways in which the teddies were used often seemed to be similar to Winnicott's (1951) description of a transitional object as an object representing aspects of the child. Staff would respond to the child's use of a teddy based upon an understanding of what the teddy represented for a particular child. The use of a transitional object by a child can be a significant development in the capacity to manage his feelings and anxieties.

We often think of teddies as transitional objects (Dockar-Drysdale 1980). In this case, the child is using the teddy as something to help him bridge the gap between his internal and external world. For example, if he has a wish for provision from his carer and the carer is not available, he may create an object that represents his carer. This object is then invested with some of the good qualities of his carer, which enables him to tolerate the separation. Often infants will find an object that is connected to the carer in some way, or given by the carer, such as a blanket. Some children have a greater need for a transitional object than others, and some stick to one specific object.

We need to be careful in a group setting that we do not encourage an institutional culture to develop around this. If a transitional object helps a child manage a feeling of frustration and separation anxiety, his carer could be tempted to encourage him to use the object as a way of keeping him settled, rather than have to work with the feelings. The problem develops when a carer who is struggling to be emotionally involved encourages the child to use the object as a substitute for the involvement rather than as a symbol of it. The object is then being used to fill rather than bridge a gap.

The most significant thing about a transitional object is that the child has found and created it himself. The carer will recognize the importance of the object for the child and support his use of it. An example in our setting could be our response to a child going to school and feeling separation anxiety. One approach is for the adult to become emotionally involved with the child and through empathy help him to think about and manage his feelings. If the child receives this support, he may be able to find ways of recognizing and managing these feelings. For example, he may be able to talk about his feelings or use an object, which helps him to hold onto the sense of an internalized 'good object'. If the adult reacts too anxiously to the child's anxiety by quickly trying to pacify the feeling, this will not help him to recognize his feelings and find his own ways of managing them. A pacifier such as a dummy or teddy used in this way is being used to deny separation and rather than symbolically representing the 'good object', the teddy becomes a concrete substitute.

Another use of teddies can be as a self-object. In this case, the child uses the teddy to represent part of himself. A child might use the teddy to communicate his feelings or to be looked after. This can be a positive way for a child who feels vulnerable to receive attention in a way that is slightly indirect and less threatening. If his teddy is invested with this type of meaning, then the way we respond to his teddy will be as if we were responding to him. This work needs to be thought about carefully. For example, an overemphasis on this approach could feed into a feeling that we are unable to really care for the child, that is, it really is too threatening and difficult.

There are many different ways of working with children's feelings about separation. As unintegrated children begin to evolve, the sense of self grows and hence a feeling of separation. A transitional space develops between the child and his carers, and between his inner and external worlds. The way in which we work with this development is likely to become an aspect of our culture.

The therapeutic task with emotionally unintegrated children

A clear approach to the treatment of emotionally unintegrated children was developed, shaped largely through the work of Dockar-Drysdale. Much of the theory was documented in her books and by other key staff in papers and working notes. This is a review and summary of the approach and looks at how some of the concepts and approaches discussed above can be organized within the structured approach of a primary house.

Theoretical focus for the treatment approach

Emotionally unintegrated children lived in houses that were called 'primary' houses. The aim of the treatment task is to facilitate the emotional growth of unintegrated children towards integration. The focus for this is the provision of primary experience for each child, in a dependant attachment with a specific member of the care team. For a child to become emotionally dependant on an adult and receive primary provision, he must experience an attuned level of preoccupation from that adult and the whole environment. This high level of attentiveness and receptivity towards a child is representative of primary maternal preoccupation. It recognizes a child's need to:

- have his communications contained (received, thought about and understood) (Bion 1962);
- be protected from impingement (intolerable disruption and stimulation) (Dockar-Drysdale 1960b);

- receive individual adaptation to need (Dockar-Drysdale 1961);
- have opportunity for reparation and contributing to others (Dockar-Drysdale 1953; Winnicott 1963);
- experience reality in manageable doses so that he is able to develop a sense of a boundary between himself and others (Winnicott 1964).

The main structures for this approach are the:

- high level of consistency and continuity provided by the staff cover plan, the roles of carer and back-up carer and systems of communication;
- bedtime visits, waking-up and care from the focal-carer and back-up carer;
- individual meetings with a specific adult;
- group meetings;
- adaptation to need through the provision of 'special things'.

Consistency of care and treatment

A focal-carer is assigned to a child taking into consideration his needs. For example, whether a male or female is most suitable. The role of the focal-carer is to provide the child with an opportunity for attachment. This is achieved through reliable provision and by becoming emotionally attuned. The focal-carer will ensure that the child's care needs are met and will be the person who regularly wakes the child, puts him to bed and spends individual time with him. The back-up person will work in tandem with the focal-carer and look after the child during the focal-carer's absence. The original aim was for the back-up person to be a second adult, providing continuity in a child's care and creating a three-way relationship with the focal-carer. Though there needs to be a number of staff sharing the back-up role, we should provide as much consistency over time as is possible. Each child should always know who is looking after him each day. There could be a second adult, who has a specific role in a child's treatment. For different reasons a triangular relationship, between a child, his carer and another adult, can be a key part of treatment. Where this is the case, it is necessary for the team to understand this role and plan how best to support it.

A primary house provides a child with the opportunity of relating to a number of adults within and outside of the house in different ways. This enables a child to try out different types of relationships, to gain different experiences, and to experience separation by moving towards and away from different adults. It is also necessary for a child to have a range of adults available to him because his previous experiences may have made it difficult for him to relate to certain adults. The communication between adults enables the whole of the child to be kept in mind and held together – this is as if the fragmented bits of him are being put together. It also ensures the primary provision is focused and pushed towards the specific adult.

Group meetings provide:

- a child with the opportunity of taking a step towards others and experiencing separation;
- the adult with an opportunity of presenting a child with external reality in a supportive setting;
- an opportunity for a child to experience containment in a group setting;
- an opportunity for reparation and contributing to others.

The language we use to describe the work around these structures

'Carer' is the word used most often to describe the specific adult assigned to a child for a dependant attachment. The word 'carer' encompasses what primary provision is about. However, all of the adults care for the children and to have one 'carer' could exclude the caring role of other adults. The term 'focal-carer' most accurately describes the role of the specific adult. This term could be used with social workers, parents, in meetings and on records. It could also be explained to children from time to time, though 'carer' would be acceptable for everyday use. Often we use the phrase 'the person who looks after a child'. This fits with primary provision, though again it should not exclude the potential caring role of other adults.

The word 'boy' is always used in relation to children and 'adult' or 'grown-up' in relation to adults. Boy defines gender and has a static meaning. We admit boys into the Community, boys leave the Community and even come back to visit after leaving, sometimes with their own boys or girls! The term 'young person' gives a greater sense of a person evolving. 'Adult' and 'child' give a sense of two quite separate and distinct things. At what point does a child become an adult? Do the words add to a sense of a gulf between the two? The word 'adult' suggests a person who has grown into something and gives a sense of development. We should consider the words we use in these areas and what our motivations are.

The role of focal-carer and back-up carer

A predominant need for children who have suffered trauma and emotional deprivation during the first years of life is for a primary attachment similar to that normally experienced by an infant with a parent. The need for continuity in this attachment means that a structure is needed to ensure the child's needs are met during the primary attachment figure's absence and to provide a third person in the relationship. The role of back-up carer evolved and began with a concept developed by Dockar-Drysdale.

Initially Dockar-Drysdale (1960a) conceptualized the role of 'catalyst'. The following extracts from her work give a sense of the role's purpose.

> People working with what I have described as pre-neurotic children are extremely vulnerable, because of the tremendous personal involvement necessary in working with regressions and progressions. At certain points in this kind of work, the adult is as undefended in relation to the child as the mother is in relation to her baby. It is painful and difficult to discard such defenses even for the time being, and can only be relatively safe in a highly protected environment. The mother–baby unity is vulnerable in the same way. This unity is protected (all being well) by a barrier against stimuli provided ideally by the father, or failing him, by other protecting people and by the home milieu itself. The therapist–child involvement must also be protected by a supporting person (whom I find convenient to call the catalyst) and by the therapeutic milieu. The catalyst is the person who can be used by both the grown-up and the child, remaining constant and unchanging, and thus facilitating deep changes in the involvement of grown-up and child. (p.43)

Also, from the glossary to *Therapy and Consultation in Child Care:*

> *Catalyst* is a term borrowed from chemistry. A catalyst enables a chemical reaction to take place. A third person may facilitate a reaction or an interaction between the child who is the consumer and the person who is the provider in a primary experience. (1993b, p.157)

From these extracts, it can be seen that the provision of primary experience in a focal-carer–child relationship needs the supportive involvement of a third person. In practice, the role of the third person can include managing anxieties and protecting the relationship, thus enabling the grown-up and child to risk vulnerability and to survive powerful feelings. At times, the catalyst can intervene to reduce the intensity of feelings between the two, perhaps taking on a 'bad' object role. This provides an outlet for negative feelings from the child and carer, which helps the focal-carer–child relationship to feel safer emotionally. Later in the relationship, the catalyst can play a key role in supporting and encouraging the separation between the focal-carer and child. The emphasis is on supporting the provision made by the focal-carer. In the cases of the most unintegrated children, the continuity of provision from both the carer and catalyst is central, as the child is not ready to experience gaps and separation. However, even at this stage our aim is to focus the provision on the focal-carer. The catalyst can help to bridge the gaps until the child has internalized reliable provision.

Over time, the concept of back-up carer has developed. The role of this person has become focused on providing continuity in the carer's absence. This has been based on the principle that children should always have a clear and reliable sense of who is looking after them. In more recent years, as hours of work have reduced it has become difficult to plan a consistent focal-carer and back-up carer for each child. In most cases, it is necessary for a child to have at least two back-up carers.

There is variation in how the back-up role is viewed. In some cases, it is mainly limited to the bedtime visit and waking a child up. In others, it is felt that care and preoccupation are provided throughout the carer's absence. Where a back-up carer has become particularly significant, there is more of a continuing three-way relationship similar to the catalyst role.

In the light of these changes, how do we meet the needs of children in the present context and what is the appropriate model? The catalyst type of role is important in our therapeutic approach. The 'third person' is provided in a number of ways. The whole team could be involved in supporting the focal-carer–child relationship. It could also be one specific person. This may evolve naturally and could be any of the team. A consistent back-up person is likely to take on the role. A manager keeping an overview of the whole group may often be in this role.

We need to think about the type of third person support each focal-carer–child relationship requires and include this in the treatment plan. The catalyst role does not have to be provided by the back-up carer. In this sense, it does not seem so necessary that the back-up carer is always the same person. However, unintegrated children in particular do need a level of care that is consistent and provided by a small number of adults. This helps give a child a sense of order and continuity. It also enables the adults to keep in close communication, so they are able to keep the whole child in mind. Two adults working closely together can meet the need for continuity in care and provision most effectively. The need will continue until the child has internalized a sense of reliable provision, and is ready to cope with gaps and experiences of separation. From this point of view, we should try to plan our resources so that it is the most unintegrated children who have just one back-up carer.

The importance of food in a therapeutic setting

In work with emotionally deprived children, the provision of food is clearly of central importance (see Hancock, Simmons and Whitwell 1990). We need to give food much attention to ensure the approach is based upon deep understanding, rather than only on what appear to be common sense views on healthy eating.

How do we understand a child's behavior around food? For example, if a child seems to be constantly eating? In this case, one possibility is that the child is eating to deny feelings, to keep feelings in rather than let them out. This could also be a kind of soothing to make things feel better. If he is doing this, should we let him continue? This will need thinking about in terms of how can we help the child with those feelings. For example, we could suggest to him that he has had a lot to eat, but still seems upset and it may be better that we try to think about that with him.

Another question could be whether the child is eating in a way that feels like self-provision, excluding any relationships, or is taking the food within the context of a relationship? Soothing or comforting through food could be valuable to him, if the food is provided for him by an adult. Greed about food provided by an adult could be seen as a move away from self-provision to allowing his needs to be met by someone else. For mistrustful children this is a positive development. A deprived child may be quite excited and demanding about this to discover if his needs really can be met and for how long. An unintegrated infant has illusions of infinity, which his mother allows him to have by the way she manages the environment around him. It is normal for a short period in early child development that the infant has little awareness of limits or anxiety about there being enough. There will be times where children here need to have similar experiences. There are also limits imposed by the reality of different situations. Some of these limits or restrictions are related to economics and organization. As long as we are clear what the reasons for these limits are, they can also be valuable to children.

Sometimes children will reject food and not want to eat. Again, it is helpful to think about this in a similar way. Is the rejection within a relationship or to exclude relationships? Is the child trying to find out whether he will be punished or whether we notice he is not eating? Will we be bothered or concerned, or will we force him to eat?

Food can have associations for children that are related to their experiences of trauma and abuse. Some children feel anxious about having meals provided for them and feel the need to be more in control of what they eat. A child may do this by asking for the same food every mealtime, such as a sandwich, or by taking from a snack tin before or after meals. We should be careful that this is not reinforcing self-provision, while also respecting the child's anxiety. If a child is going to a snack tin, it is better that adults notice what he is doing and he knows this, rather than him, literally, feeling he has provided the food himself. It is the relationship within which the provision of food takes place that is the central aspect of the provision rather than the food itself. Therapeutic provision involves a child receiving something that is connected to and reflects his own needs. For instance, he feels:

> I am getting this because it is what I need; my carer knows this and wants to give it to me. If she wants to give it to me, it must be good and I must be good.

Adaptations can be a specific type of food provision. This is where a child asks for a special kind of food from his carer, which is provided reliably over a period and normally privately. This can be a key part of their relationship and is representative of early maternal provision.

Mealtimes

Mealtimes are central to care in a residential setting and have particular significance in the therapeutic treatment of emotionally traumatized and deprived children (see Menzies Lyth 1985; Rose 1987, 1990). Inevitably, due to the importance of this and the emotional issues involved, mealtimes are demanding and potentially rewarding events. Constant attention by the staff team to what this involves is essential to ensure the successful holding of mealtimes in the daily routine.

The provision of food is closely associated with primary provision. Paying attention to the way we provide a mealtime can make it a potentially nourishing experience both emotionally and physically. This includes paying attention to the quality of food, how it is bought and cooked, how the dining room is decorated, how the dining table is laid and the adults' general attitude to the mealtime. In all of these areas, we should consider the meaning for the children and how they are involved.

Group mealtimes, where each group eats together at set times during the day, are practical to organize and provide a sense of reliable provision. If we had the resources, this sense of reliability could also be provided by cooking for children separately at different times, as long as we responded to need. Fixed mealtimes in themselves do not meet the need for reliable provision. If the expectations of mealtimes are too rigid, they will interfere or conflict with other needs that coincide with the mealtime.

In primary houses, the individual needs of children at mealtimes require careful thought. This will be over things like who sits where (children and adults), whether a child is served or serves himself, and any individual details such as how a child likes his food prepared. Emotionally traumatized and deprived children are likely to have all manner of anxieties related to their own experiences around food, eating in groups and being provided for in general. During the mealtime, a child may need a high level of attentiveness and support to manage the experience. Children who are at a pre-group stage in their emotional development will at times need almost undivided attention. It helps some children to have some meals on their own with an adult. If there are two or three children like this at a mealtime and adults are trying to eat at the same time, the conflicting needs can generate high levels of anxiety. In this case, the adult may be more able to help a child with his anxieties, if she does not have to eat at the same time. If the adult feels dissatisfied with her own experience, the child could pick this up in a way that is unhelpful to him. Children who need high levels of attention could eat with adults who were not also eating, while children who are more ready for a group experience could eat together with adults. This may provide children with the type of experience that is appropriate to their different emotional stages of development.

Mealtimes provide a social group experience for all children, as well as meeting individual needs within that. Mealtimes can be used as an opportunity for communication. A routine where all children are expected to eat together and finish the mealtime together can help to create the mealtime as a key aspect of the therapeutic approach. Emotionally traumatized and deprived children need positive experiences with a beginning, middle and end.

Food and children's physical weight

Due to the importance of food in the overall therapeutic approach, the issue of healthy eating and physical weight needed to be considered within this context. At times in their development, children can gain in weight significantly. Sometimes this seems more related to a child's age and changes in his physical growth. At other times, reasons for weight gain are mostly emotional. For example, eating for comfort and to get away from difficult feelings. At points in work with a child, the eating is linked to primary provision and the relationship with his carer. If a child has been severely deprived and reaches a point where he is able to trust enough to have his needs met, he may feel greedy and want to have as much as he can. This is a hopeful sign and can be seen in some cases as the conversion of delinquency (self-provision) to oral excitement. In this situation, we should nurture the feeling of excitement about food and be careful not to do anything that could lead the child to feel he is bad or that it is wrong to have these feelings. He will feel quite vulnerable and may have underlying anxieties such as he does not deserve good things or if he has something good it will only be taken away.

Children who gain weight often lose it as they move on in their emotional development. Where we do have a particular concern about a child's health, we should seek medical advice to ensure we are working appropriately with health matters. We try to provide a balanced diet, so that there is not an overabundance of cakes and sugary foods. We need to think carefully about provision and keep it focused, so that real need is being met and not just endless demand. It is appropriate to manage children's eating within limits. For example, at bedtime we offer limited choices of food and drink, and at other times we put some limits on quantity. If the child is eating continuously to avoid feeling something, he will find it very difficult to stop. If we support him with this, he may be able to acknowledge and think about some of his underlying feelings.

If a child does put weight on, he could feel worried about being 'fat'. If he feels vulnerable, his self-esteem is also likely to be fragile. He will be sensitive to anxiety about his appearance and any perceived criticism and comments from others. We should be attentive to these concerns and try to understand what the worry is about. For example, there may be a genuine issue related to the child's weight that we can help him do something about. This can help give him a sense of control and improve his self-esteem. In another case, the child's weight may not be an actual problem, but he has low self-esteem and anxieties about eating. He could be testing to see if we think it is okay for him to enjoy his food and to want us to provide for him. Deprived children may have been given messages like 'you must not eat too much or you'll get fat' or 'you're greedy'. Deprived parents or carers can find it difficult to see children eating and enjoying their food. Feelings of envy can be evoked and an anxiety that the child's need will be overwhelming.

As well as thinking about the lack of self-esteem and whatever it is focused on, we can help a child's self-esteem by paying attention to things he can do well and feel good about.

The provision of food and drink for children and adults

Providing food for traumatized and deprived children is a demanding task, as it requires a trusting relationship for a child to accept and value the food he is being offered. In providing the food, the adult is meeting both the physical and emotional needs of the child. At the same time, the adult will have her own needs related to food and these can be evoked powerfully when involved in this area of work. The child will be observant of the adult's feelings around food, what she is providing for the child and herself. As food is so central to the primary provision needs of traumatized and deprived children, a clear approach is essential.

One of the main principles about the provision of food is that it should be good enough for everyone. The children often have anxiety about the food we provide and accepting the provision from someone. Normally an adult cooking a meal for a group will also eat the meal, partly to give the message that the food is okay and enjoyable. To not eat the meal can raise anxieties about why it has not been eaten. It is imaginable that these anxieties could be worked with. For example, the adult may not eat so that she could pay more attention to a child. However, to eat something different (which is not on offer to everyone) at the same time would be inappropriate unless for special reasons like, for example, medical ones but this should be made known.

The house should provide a good enough range of food and drink for everyone to have a choice within that. A house team needs to agree and decide what a reasonable and practical range is. Special provision outside of this should only be made for cultural and medical reasons, or as an adaptation in a child's treatment. If adults take their own food and drink to work, this could be quite tantalizing to children, especially if it is something that is not provided for them. It may also give the message that the house provision is not sustaining in some way and could be felt like self-provision.

Children's visits during bedtime

Bedtime became a focal point for nurture and meeting a child's regressed needs. This was an appropriate time for children to receive individual provision in a planned way. Bedtime for this group of children would also tend to be a difficult time with anxieties to do with separation and possibly trauma associated with earlier childhood experiences. The need for emotional holding as well as the opportunity for meeting specific need led to a high level of thought, assessment and planning about this time of day.

The bedtime routine in primary houses

Supper begins at 8.30pm and ends at 9pm. Children may be changed for supper. During supper food is provided while a story is read, or games are played or a video watched. After supper, children are helped to their rooms. A child will have a visit with his carer for about 10 minutes. During this time, a child will play a game or have a story and will be offered a small snack and drink. There are rules about what and how much a child has. An adaptation may also be provided during a visit. All children are tucked in by their carer at 10pm when lights are turned out.

In the secondary house for emotionally integrated children, supper is between 9pm and 9.30pm. Food is provided for children and adults who may sit together talking, playing games or watching television. During the visit, the child and adult talk together or play a game. Mostly children are provided with drinks for their visit. Children are expected to settle in their rooms by 10.30pm. Children do not have adaptations.

The relevance of bedtime visits in the therapeutic approach

Visits are used as an important part of primary provision to meet individual needs. They provide an opportunity for localized provision. The provision of adaptations, food, drink, and everything a child and adult do together during a visit develops out of their relationship and is highly individualized. This in itself provides a routine, which can be comforting to a child. The emphasis should be on creating a calm and settling atmosphere at these times. It is not a good time for opening up new work about the day's difficulties, though a child may need matters or concerns he has to be referred to and acknowledged. For example, it could be helpful for a back-up carer to acknowledge the carer's absence. A child's carer or back-up carer should be generally tuned into his feelings and the preoccupation provides a context for the visit. The visit provides a focus for and is representative of the relationship between a child and his carer. It represents the emotional containment provided by the carer and the continuity of provision, which survives the child's destructive impulses. Suppertime can provide a similar experience for the group as a whole. For instance, if the whole group sits around together listening to a story with food, this not only provides a feeding type of experience, it also gives the reassuring message that we are all here together at the end of the day.

If we are unable to provide a child with a visit one evening due to other difficulties and time constraints, he could feel this is a negative reflection of him and we are punishing him. For instance, 'I'm bad, so I'm losing good things' or 'I'm losing good things, so I must be bad.' It is central to a child's treatment that we should expect to provide a visit and the carer should be supported wherever possible in doing this. If a child's carer is feeling overwhelmed she may be liable to overprovide on the visit to appease the child or to deal with feelings of guilt towards him. In relation to these points, there should be consistent limits around all aspects of the visit. In each house the carers should hold in mind a clear sense of the purpose of the visit and details such as how much time to spend and what can be provided. The consistency within a house is essential if the provision is to be effective. These limits also help to manage a localized regression so that it feels like a complete experience, with a beginning, middle and end.

Sometimes a child may reject his visit or try to spoil it. While we will try to work with this so the child is able to have his visit, there can be a value and purpose to the rejecting behavior. Inevitably, children will push against these limits and may compare visits with each other. Some children might focus on the exact time and length of the visits. The feelings involved in these matters need working with rather than responding to defensively. It is easy but unhelpful to become drawn into arguments over who has had the longest visit. Visits should be organized so carers have enough time to do them and are not too anxious about having time.

The visit can also make a link to the next day. For emotionally unintegrated children this link can be held in the carer's mind and for children who are more integrated it may be helpful for the carer to refer to it.

Providing opportunities for primary provision and matters related to privacy and safety

When spending individual time with a child, it was not unusual to have the room door closed. Partly this was to give a sense of privacy and individual space and to protect a child from feeling vulnerable to the intrusion of other children. In recent years, it was felt that the vulnerability of a child and adult being alone in a room with the door closed also creates another type of vulnerability for the child and adult.

There are three regular situations where an adult spends time with a child on his own in a room with the door closed: a child's individual meeting, his bedtime visit and his wash. These occasions are a regular part of a house culture. Most children in primary houses have a wash (face and hands) and teeth clean with their carer in the morning and evening. All children, except those who require physical assistance, take a bath on their own with the door locked.

Emotionally unintegrated children have been deprived of primary provision during infancy. Physical care is a central part of the provision. Because of this deprivation, the unintegrated children we work with have little internalized experience of care, including physical care. Without this experience, it is not possible to care properly for oneself or others. As the children we work with are not actually infants, the treatment we provide needs to recognize this reality. The children need provision that is representative of early missed experiences, which can be internalized by the child. This distinction is a key aspect of the provision and helps to keep in mind the reality of a child's deprivation and the losses involved in that, rather than trying to substitute or compensate for the deprivation. The latter could lead to a denial of his early deprivation and losses.

A wash is one way in which a child can choose to have a localized experience that is representative of early physical care. It is a form of localized regression where the boundaries around the experience are quite clear and safe, that is, face and hand washing, teeth cleaning and hair combing. Where these experiences are meaningful to a child, the attention of the adult and at times the play that can be involved is also representative of the parent-infant relationship. When a child feels that he needs these types of experiences and when he begins to believe that it is possible for someone to meet these needs, he is faced with the risk of allowing himself to be dependant. This faces him with the possibility of being let down or rejected. It is important that his vulnerability is understood by the adults involved and that the adult ensures that any provision offered is completely reliable. Both the child's vulnerability and the provision need a degree of protection from disruption and impingement. In relation to this, it is understandable that a child (or adult) may wish to close the door while he has his wash, so there is no risk of disruption particularly from other children. It is also usual that children will enviously attack and try to spoil each other's provision.

The solution of closing the door creates another problem to the situation. The child and adult in a closed room together are both vulnerable. The child is vulnerable to the adult misusing the privacy and intimacy in a way that is unhelpful or at worst abusive. The adult is also vulnerable to the child's manipulation of the situation, for example, the child could make allegations against the adult. If a child has been abused in the past when left on his own with an adult, he may feel quite unsafe in these situations. On the one hand, we can protect him from this anxiety and risk by not allowing him to be in these situations. On the other hand, we need to be careful not to reinforce his belief that he will always be abused if left on his own with an adult. The level of concern and anxiety that has developed over these matters not only questions whether the practice of closing doors is contrary to child protection, it also makes it difficult to maintain the provision without being distracted.

It is possible to continue with a child's wash as a part of provision, but by also changing the culture around it. The door is being used in a concrete way to represent a protective boundary. The door then takes on an illusory quality. The child's wash is not actually protected from disruption by the closed door. The same would apply to the child's bedtime visit. These provisions can be and often are disrupted. If we did not rely so much on the closed door then the message from adults about respecting personal space and individual need would have to be worked on more explicitly. For example, more emphasis could be put on knocking first. To reinforce the sense of safety it is helpful to develop a culture where adults check on each other from time to time to see that everything is okay. The sense that an adult may pop her head around the door would make the child and adult less vulnerable. It should also be possible for the child to feel trustful that the adults are working together to meet his needs.

The practice of leaving a door slightly ajar could be adopted for meetings, visits and washes. These changes need working on carefully and thoughtfully. The idea of a closed door and what it represents may be significant to children and adults and a change in this area could raise anxiety. One dilemma may be where a child actually requests an adult to close a door for privacy. We can respond to this by acknowledging his wish, but also by explaining to him that we will keep the door ajar as we think it is the safest way of doing things.

While the most important aspect of safety lies in the way we work together as a team, specific aspects of the culture such as closing doors do add in a degree of vulnerability. It is difficult to say exactly how changes we introduce will impact on our culture. For example, does having a door slightly ajar rather than closed affect the quality of communication during an individual meeting? Possibly the most critical factor is how the adults work with and manage the anxieties involved.

Chapter 3

Therapeutic Task with Emotionally Integrated Children – Theory and Practice

As the Cotswold Community developed its understanding of emotional integration and unintegration and used Dockar-Drysdale's (1970a, 1970b, 1990b) 'need assessment' to help classify the needs of children, it was decided that unintegrated and integrated children would be separated into different houses. Unintegrated children lived in a primary house and integrated children in a secondary house. As unintegrated children became integrated, there was the option of a move to the secondary house for a further stage of treatment. Occasionally an integrated child would be referred to the Community and move straight into the secondary house. The approach to therapeutic work with children who have suffered severe trauma but who have reached emotional integration needs to be focused clearly on the child's stage of development. This chapter clarifies some of the key issues involved in the approach.

Working with fragilely integrated children

The treatment task

As a child becomes integrated, there is a growing expectation of him as a separate individual and his capacity for managing himself. Children are expected to discuss their feelings more openly and clearly. There is a clear expectation that a child is responsible for his own choices and actions. The therapeutic aim is to enable fragilely integrated children to consolidate their integration, developing their capacity to manage themselves in relation to others and to be responsible for their own choices.

A child's sense of his own identity grows through the opportunities he has for:

- general interaction in the care setting;
- considering his own and others' experiences and opinions;
- receiving feedback about himself from others;
- making positive contributions to others;
- being acknowledged and thought about by others;
- making choices and negotiating with others;
- working through what he has experienced.

These processes help a child to recognize his own individuality and the differences between people. Children who have the opportunity to do this with their own peers can gradually learn how to manage themselves in relation to others, developing social skills which can be used in building relationships. This work will involve a lot of experimentation and learning from experience. It will also be happening within the context of developing adolescence and puberty. This is a new development and not just a continuation of integration, and brings its own matters that will need working on. We also need to recognize and acknowledge that once a child is 16, his legal status in terms of being in care and his rights change.

As a child develops towards integration, he will increasingly be expected to consider himself in relation to external reality. This will progress to the point where he leaves and has to be responsible for himself as a young adult. In this respect the learning of social skills, developing the capacity to look after himself and the ability to live within the constraints of an external set of rules are core aims of treatment. The group living context is central to the therapeutic task. The house culture, including all of its daily routines, events and activities, expectations about how people live together, rules and boundaries are all part of this. To some extent, this culture will develop out of the group, led by the adults but not imposed in the same way that a primary house culture is. Negotiation and choice are key aspects of the work. Some aspects of daily living will be nonnegotiable to everyone, some will have more room for negotiation and choice to the group as a whole, while others will vary individually. The amount of negotiating space that can be managed will be different for each child. A child should be allowed enough space so that he can stretch himself, try new things out, with the possibility of succeeding or failing in a way that he can learn from the experience. Some children will push for more space than the adults think is appropriate. This can be worked on with adults taking a firm line if necessary. Other children will resist taking responsibility and will need to be given space to manage themselves.

The relationship between a child and specific adult and the language we use to describe it

Fragilely integrated children need to be held in mind reliably by a parental figure. In particular, when a child first moves in he often needs a lot of care and attention to his individual needs. Over time, the adult who is providing this becomes more like a keyworker keeping an overview of the child's treatment. The child's ability to look after himself also develops over time. While the keyworker relationship provides care, a child's care is not focused wholly onto this relationship. The word 'carer' can be associated with the type of emotional holding and physical handling that Winnicott (1960b) describes the infant as needing, a kind of nursing. In this sense, 'carer' is more suited to the work of a primary house. On the other hand, care can mean detailed thought and attention that is appropriate to this task, as well as the fact that young people continue to need physical care to varying degrees.

In healthy development a child will become emotionally integrated after one to two years of life. The children with whom the Community works tend to become integrated between 12 and 15 years. Some of them will then soon find themselves living as young adults with the associated responsibility. From this point of view, the term 'keyworker' is more suitable as it shifts the emphasis from being cared for in a rather passive way, while retaining the sense of a central involved adult. It suggests more of a two-way relationship.

We may feel ambivalence about seeing 12- to 15-year-old children as 'emotional toddlers' or young adults or men. We may feel anxiety and guilt about moving fragilely integrated children on, especially if we are thinking of them as toddlers. Could the continued use of the word 'child' reflect a reluctance to let children really grow up? If we are overidentified with primary care, we could be resistant to using words such as 'keyworker' and 'young person'.

The therapeutic approach with fragilely integrated children is based on psychological and social aspects of the individual. It is a model that utilizes the therapeutic potential inherent in the interpersonal interactions within the social milieu, and the interpersonal and intrapsychic experience of the person (child and worker). This approach is similar to the psychosocial care model described by the Cassel Hospital (Kennedy, Heymans and Tischler 1987). Psychosocial practice attempts to create an environment that turns experience into learning, for both clients and staff. This practice utilizes domestic and recreational aspects of living, and the interactions between children and staff, as a focus of enquiry and treatment.

The structures to facilitate the task

As discussed, much of the work takes place around the daily experience of living together as a group. Group meetings are used as a focal point for this work. Young people are encouraged to see themselves as part of a group and this is most clear when the whole group meets together. The emphasis of the therapeutic approach shifts from the individual in relation to one other or a small group to the individual in relation to the whole group.

One possibility for the structure of group meetings is a daily house meeting, which will take place from Monday to Friday after tea. The meeting could have a minimum duration of 20 minutes and maximum of one hour. The minimum of 20 minutes is to encourage the group to engage with each other rather than take flight by not meeting at all. The upper limit of one hour gives room for working in greater depth but does not create such a rigid structure that other aspects of living together are greatly restricted. How the group decides when to end the meeting will be part of the group's work and is quite appropriate to the task.

The meeting will be an opportunity for anyone to raise anything relevant to the experience of living together as a group – with the aim of developing open communication and facilitating the task as we have described previously. The group meeting is in itself a specific therapeutic tool and the approach to it should reflect the way the group lives and works together. The group meeting is symbolically representative of and a focus for the daily life of the group.

It is positive for young people to spend time on their own with an adult as a way of ending the day. Without opening up further work, it is possible to round the day off in a way that acknowledges events of the day and anything relevant to the next day. It is also a space where a young person can enjoy some individual time. Nighttime seems particularly appropriate for this, as it is a time for separating from the group and being alone. It also acts as a useful time for the adults to be in touch with and tuned in to each young person. The main aim is that each young person has some reliable time with an adult before settling down. It does not have to be with the same adult in such a regular pattern, for the same amount of time every night, with provision of food and drink. The emphasis on food should be more connected to supper and the time before going to bed. The visit could be from any of the adults working, though the young person's keyworker would be involved most regularly. To ensure that this time is valued and reliable it may be necessary for there to be a pattern to it.

However, it helps to remember the reason for this and not to slip into recreating primary provision. There are possibilities, on the one hand, of leaving a young person on his own too much and, on the other, of being involved in a way that encourages regression rather than separation. Feelings for young people and adults can swing between neglect and indulgence. How these matters are dealt with and a steady path maintained, where adults and young people are not drawn to an extreme in either direction, is central to the task.

For example, if a young person's keyworker is away and he is provided with a back-up person, does this provide continuity of care or does it fill in the space the young person has for thinking about absence and developing his capacity for managing himself at those times? In reality, the two things may not be exclusive but we need to think carefully about such questions. It is important to think why a young person wants or does not want something from an adult and the reasons why an adult feels or does not feel the need to provide something.

Working with emotionally integrated and unintegrated children together

Children placed in primary houses were assessed during the referral stage as emotionally unintegrated. The task of a primary house was specifically focused on meeting the needs of these children. The whole culture of the house was orientated around this task. When a child developed towards emotional integration, there was a need to adapt the approach to his needs while managing the impact of this on the other children. The matters involved are relevant to work with groups of children who are individually at significantly different levels of emotional stages of development.

Some of the concerns involved in this situation

There is a risk of ignoring the needs of a more emotionally integrated child in a primary house. It is easy to leave him to get on and manage while the adults attend to the more needy children. This could be experienced as a sort of secondary deprivation, where the child is expected to cope with too much while his carers are busy or preoccupied with other things. How does the child get an experience of being with his own peer group? Should he spend some time with peer groups outside of the house, or more time at home with his family?

How far can any house meet a spectrum of need, for example, from the very unintegrated to the integrated? Each house has a specialized task and resources designed to perform that task. If the task is stretched, there will inevitably be wider matters and a range of difficulties to work with. For example, for fragilely integrated children there is the difficulty of separating from primary provision and holding onto newly emerging feelings of concern rather than taking flight from them. Being surrounded by children who are receiving primary provision and often unable to feel any concern can act as a regressive pull. The fragilely integrated child's fear of disintegrating can easily be accentuated. It will also be difficult for him to manage himself in relation to a number of unintegrated children who have little sense of identity and personal boundaries. The integrated child may feel powerful or omnipotent in this position. This dynamic can then become a defense that is used by the unintegrated as well as the integrated children. The unintegrated children could use the delinquent excitement involved as a form of self-provision.

Given the deprivation and abuse that many children here have experienced, they are also vulnerable to attacker-victim and seducer-predator type of relationships. The potential differences of power between integrated and unintegrated children could be a major risk to safety. Another possibility is that the integrated children who are being weaned off primary provision, rather than resist this, enviously attack the provision they see being provided for other children. This could create an anxiety for the unintegrated children that makes it feel less safe for them to regress and allow their more infantile needs to be met. Similarly, in a house where the task is about consolidating development and moving forwards, the presence of a more unintegrated child may hold the group back. In addition, he could feel threatened by such a demanding situation and attack the functioning of the group.

The expectations we have of a child in whatever situation will make a difference. For instance, if an emotionally integrated child is expected to play like a young child he may feel belittled and threatened as if his needs are not understood. In reality, the importance of the group culture in each house makes it difficult for there to be many exceptions to the rule. The culture will be predominantly focused to meet the needs of children at a specific stage of development. However, it is not to say the problems of working with a diverse mix of developmental stages are in themselves impossible. There can be a benefit by having a wider range of developmental stages in the group. If the difficulties and conflicts involved can be tackled, this can help develop children's understanding of each other and themselves. Children can look backwards and forwards at their development. Without this, there can be a tendency towards stagnation. The resources required to deal with the difficulties involved are substantial and it can be more efficient to separate integrated and unintegrated children. Once we are clear of the reasons why children are separated in this way, then there is the question of how the process of separation is used as part of the therapeutic process.

How may an integrated child benefit from being in a primary house? He could need more primary care to consolidate his development and be more able to use this in an environment where primary care is openly accepted in the group. He may be integrated but still feel very young. On the other hand, some children can more easily accept localized provision if there is an expectation to function at other times. In this respect, some children are able to use localized provision in a secondary house.

If an integrated child needs primary care, could this be achieved in a good family environment? The wish for primary care could also be an attempt to meet a need that could be better treated through individual therapy.

Criteria for assessing whether a child is ready to move on

Assessing when a child is ready to move on is a complex task and one that needs a clear structure and process to help prevent decisions being made for the wrong reasons. The majority of children would move from primary to secondary house before leaving altogether. The principles discussed below can be applied to matters of assessment in relation to a child's or young person's readiness to move on.

As well as the assessment process described above, there may be other factors to take into consideration in deciding whether it is right for a child to move on and how long the transitional period should be. The following factors are particularly relevant.

There could be pivotal pieces of work to complete in the primary house before the move. For example, the child may have made a recent disclosure that needs working through, or the relationship between the child and carer may need separating slowly. If, on the other hand, it seems that the child could deteriorate through staying too long in the primary house, the transition will need to be quick. Reaching emotional integration and a sense of separation can also raise paranoid feelings and anxieties related to a fear of disintegration, and inability to sustain this newly achieved state (Dockar-Drysdale 1990c, p.42). The primary house environment with its emphasis on nurture and regression can add to this internal pressure. The child might also become reactive and attack primary provision as a way of defending himself against this pressure. The achievement of integration can then feel like a negative and destructive experience for the child. These factors can vary according to the individual child and the particular culture of a house at any point in time.

A child on referral to the secondary house must show commitment to his possible placement there. Given the stage of development he has reached, it is appropriate to have an expectation that he will be responsible for his own choices. If the child is clear in saying he does not want to move to the secondary house, it would not be supportive of his development to go ahead. The child will benefit from being fully involved in the process that leads to his referral. Ideally, it is something that develops from the work with him. By the time the team have assessed a child as emotionally integrated, the child should also have begun to think about the future and the possibility of moving on. During the process of separation between a child and carer, the idea of moving on may be a theme in their work. For example, some children talk about moving on a year or more before they are ready. In this case, it would be helpful for a child's carer to take his interest seriously without implying that he may be ready for a referral. Some children can be far more reluctant to think about the possibility of moving on and adults should be careful not to collude with this anxiety by avoiding the subject.

Fragilely integrated children who have been very deprived may benefit from remaining in a primary house to have a longer experience of primary provision. The culture can feel particularly nurturing with its focus on care. A child's age could be a relevant factor. A child who is or feels relatively young could stay longer in a primary house. An older child who is adolescent is more suited to the secondary house. These factors will also vary according to the particular makeup of each group of children. For example, it could be difficult for a fragilely integrated ten-year-old to move to the secondary house if all the children there are around 15 years. What is available to a child at any point in time will influence whether he stays in a primary house, moves to the secondary house or leaves. A key aspect of the referral is assessing a child's potential to make use of the secondary house's specific therapeutic approach. For instance, there is a requirement that all children participate in group work.

We also need to be aware of underlying factors and unconscious processes. There will be pushes and pulls about the movement of children, within and between primary and secondary houses. For different reasons, we may hold onto some children for too long and push others forward too quickly. Organizational dynamics and factors also have a significant influence. It can be difficult to be aware of these and then separate them from what is really the child's need. The child's external situation needs particular attention as he reaches a possible referral. In some cases, it is more appropriate that a child leaves the Community from the primary house. In other cases, the lack of a suitable placement could weight things in favor of a move to the secondary house. We need to be careful that we do not let pressures related to these external factors distract us from making an objective assessment of a child's suitability for the secondary house.

The question of what happens to a child if he is referred but not accepted is often overlooked during the process. There will be anxiety related to this issue. For example, what if there is not a suitable external placement? Will it be appropriate for the child to continue in the primary house and, if so, for how long? If these questions are not made conscious and worked on, it is likely the anxieties come into the process indirectly. For example, the secondary house could feel undue pressure to accept a child if the possibility of an alternative has not been considered. If the adults have not worked on and anticipated this, the child may feel rejected if he is not offered a place. This work needs to be thorough to ensure it is focused on the child's needs. Similarly, the reasons for the length of transition between houses also need to be clear.

Becoming emotionally integrated and moving on

As the Cotswold Community's approach developed, it was believed that mixing emotionally unintegrated and integrated children in the same group created conflicts within the children that hindered and disrupted their progress. It was decided that integrated children would move on from the primary to the secondary house for the next stage of their treatment. This move, though designed to aid the therapeutic process, also created difficulties that could hinder and disrupt progress. This model can also be applied to a child moving from his residential home to a family or in general leaving the home.

The transition from a primary house is used as a way for a child to be weaned off primary provision and gradually to separate from his focal-carer, as well as the primary house environment in general. This process can give an opportunity to work through loss and endings in a positive way. The time involved is planned to allow enough time for this work to be done, so that when a child leaves a primary house he is ready emotionally to say goodbye and move on to the next stage of treatment.

Before a child moves, he will understand the reasons he is moving and what will happen at the next stage. He will understand that it is a developmental step and that he needs to move on from dependant attachments with primary provision and learn more about living in a group and relating to other people. The move from one house to another becomes a concrete representation of the developmental step a child is making. This step involves both positive change and loss. The move to another house based on becoming integrated is like an affirming ritual or rite of passage. This way of doing things does give a cutoff point, which can feel quite harsh if we do not build in future contact between the child and the primary house. As well as needing the continuing support and concern provided by the contact, he might need the opportunity to go back, literally, to see and experience what he has moved on from.

The move from a primary house and future contact with the child

Despite the genuine concern felt by staff towards children with whom they had worked and who had moved on, a pattern developed where future contact was often sporadic and difficult to maintain. We attempted to understand the therapeutic concerns that influence the significance of future contact. The issue of moving on and future contact is one of major importance and complexity in work with children and young people in the care system. This section is specifically related to the move from primary to secondary house within the Community, though many of the issues are relevant to future contact with all children moving on.

When a child moves on it can be difficult to organize contact between him and his previous carer. Various anxieties and difficulties can get in the way. For instance, his previous carer could be anxious about interfering with his routine in his new place, or may feel that he or his new carers will not want him to get in touch. There could be anxieties about separation and difficulty in letting go. Grown-ups in his new home may fear that the child's settling in and developing attachments could be set back by contact with his previous carer. Contact can be quite emotional for children and adults. It might be felt that cutting off literally is a way of managing these feelings. Not only is contact between the child and previous carer difficult, adults involved with the child in the two houses also often have little contact. When there has been a long relationship between a child and grown-up, it can seem odd to live close by and see little of each other.

What does the wish for contact represent? It could represent the wish to show the child a continuing sense of concern in his development and to be still involved with him in some way. If the grown-up gets something out of the contact as well, the child may get a sense that he is a person worth knowing.

When an adult from a primary house does arrange to visit a child in his new house, it can feel as if this is not work and should be done more on a social level. This could appear to the child as if he is being offered something without boundaries. If the contact cannot take place in work time, then what is its nature? The contact should take place during work time as it is a part of our professional involvement. It is also a positive message for all children in primary houses to know that adults have this continuing concern and involvement with children who move on.

The culture around contact between children and previous carers may develop better if we do it more routinely. The most straightforward way to do it could be for the child's primary house carer to approach the new house within two weeks of the move to arrange a visit, that is, if contact has not already been initiated by the child. The grown-ups in the new home can then talk about this with the child and arrange something appropriate. Depending on a child's stage of development, contact will have different meanings for him at different times. On occasions, there can be some conflicting feelings involved. If the child is resistant, he may be given a bit more space, but a visit will be arranged within the first three to four weeks. Even if the visit is difficult and the child rejects it, it shows a continuing interest in him and that he is not forgotten.

Where a child is moving to a different home within the same organization, there can be a tendency to not acknowledge the move in the way we would if the child was leaving altogether. It is important for all those involved, including the child's social worker and parents, to mark the move. This can be done by holding an introduction to the new home before the child's admission. This could take the form of a pre-admission meeting, involving the child, his social worker, his parents, and new home keyworker and manager. It could be helpful for the child's previous carer to be involved to give a sense of handing over his care and treatment. Matters about the move, the reason for it and the work to be done can be discussed and clarified. Following the meeting, arrangements can be made for other necessary visits for parents, social worker and staff to become more familiar with each other.

The referral process from a primary to secondary house

As the move from a primary to secondary house became an established part of the therapeutic task, it also became a developmental milestone and a significant event for everyone involved. The Community developed a referral process that became a clear way of determining that the child was ready for this move. Similar processes may be appropriate in settings where children and young people move on to different homes or units as part of their development.

Children placed in primary houses are assessed as emotionally unintegrated and the treatment task is to facilitate recovery so that child grows towards integration. Once integration is reached, a child may be assessed as ready to benefit from a further stage of treatment provided by the secondary house. As a child reaches this emotional milestone there is often a focus on his achievement. With the acknowledgement of his achievement, the child may feel pleased with himself. He will also benefit from the pleasure he senses the adults are deriving from the situation. It will be rewarding to the adults who have worked with him that he has evolved and benefited from this work. However, there are some questions to consider in relation to these feelings:

- Does the child sense we are happy and relieved because he is going at last?
- If we do feel pleased with our own work, do we allow the child enough space to recognize his own progress?
- Does the child feel our sense of well-being is dependant on him progressing?
- How would we feel if he had not reached this stage?
- There is likely to be ambivalence for all involved about the possible move. One child expressed this by exclaiming about his move, 'hip-hip boo-hoo'. The care taken in acknowledging our own feelings and anxieties about a referral will help the child manage his own anxieties.
- The more our sense of well-being is dependant on the progress a child makes, the greater the possibility he will develop a false-self (Winnicott 1960a) type of response to keep us happy. Our wish for progress should not impinge upon a child having space and time just to be, as well as upon our tolerance of his more difficult feelings and behavior. We should acknowledge all of the steps a child makes and not just the ones that seem the biggest.

Sometimes children moving on have the expectation of more freedom, such as being allowed to do things on their own, staying up late or going around town on their own. While it is true that part of the secondary house approach is about having more responsibility and opportunities for self-management, care must be taken during the transition not to build up these ideas in an unhelpful way. Similarly, it is unhelpful to emphasize the idea that the child's difficult behavior will be 'sorted out' in his new house. The anxieties about a transition can be difficult to work with and the lure of freedom may act as a sedative, or being 'sorted out' as a threat to manage these anxieties. A hierarchical feeling can develop in a group where each step towards emotional integration is equated with the gaining of privileges. This can encourage children to pretend to have developed to stages which they have not yet reached.

A child is normally referred to the secondary house following a period when he and the staff team have realized he is ready. Normally children will use primary provision until they no longer need it and reach a point of self-referral. The staff team will carry out a needs assessment and the child meets with a consultant to discuss the possibility of a referral. Clearly, as the child has been here for some while, we know him well and a lot of discussion can go on between different adults, in preparation for his referral. Given the anxieties that will be involved for the child, it does not seem necessary that the assessment process should be prolonged for him.

The referral assessment involves the child visiting the secondary house on a number of occasions for him to experience the house and vice versa. During the referral, a child may feel that he is on show and under observation the whole time. Throughout the whole process he has to endure this anxiety, not knowing what the outcome will be. The assessment process could be condensed into a block visit over a few days, with an initial preliminary visit. This would give everyone in the house a chance to meet the child and get to know him in the group. Condensing the time can also enable the work to be more focused. Once the assessment and decision are made, it is possible to arrange further visits. The transitional aspect of a move has been combined with the assessment process. It should be clearer and cause less anxiety for the child if these processes are separated out. It is potentially confusing for a child to be involved in a process that is transitional before a decision about a move is made.

Chapter 4

Therapeutic Education

Historically, those institutions providing therapeutic residential care and education for children with emotional difficulties have tended to focus on the emotional rather than educational needs of the children. To some extent, these needs were separated from each other and even seen to be in conflict. The Community's educational provision was initially designed for young boys who were perceived to be alienated from the education system and who would only engage if the approach used was sufficiently different from the mainstream school system. Hence, the use of the word 'poly' (polytechnic) which was clearly not 'school' and also created an emphasis on a broad rather than academic education. Evidence from national research (DH/DfEE 2000) in more recent years began to show clearly that long-term outcomes for children in care are correlated to academic educational achievements.

Throughout its history and in keeping with findings from research, the Community reviewed and improved its education provision. One of the central and most challenging tasks in residential care and education is ensuring high quality in both while maintaining the integration of care and education.

The interrelationship of education and therapy

We looked at this issue, focusing on how education and other aspects of a child's treatment fit together. We examined this particularly in the light of a more structured and planned approach to the National Curriculum, and the focus on enabling each child to reach his full educational potential.

The education of children in the Cotswold Community has developed rapidly in recent years. So far, this has not been conceptualized in relation to the theoretical base of the Community's work. There has been uncertainty as to how education fits within the psychodynamic framework. Education is increasingly led by national objectives with an emphasis on educational attainment. Young people and in particular those leaving care without qualifications can be disadvantaged after they leave care and have to make their way in the world. The approach of education varies according to the prevailing beliefs and attitudes in wider society. It is important that children are equipped in the best way possible to have opportunities and choices in that society.

There has been an underlying assumption in our work that children are referred primarily for treatment of their emotional disturbance. Children's difficulties in education are also often associated with this disturbance. There may be a concern that meeting the therapeutic needs of a child will be compromised by the demands of educational needs and requirements. For example, if a child needs to regress but is defending himself against this, is it likely education will be used to build up this defense? Sometimes anxiety is expressed that if we feed and develop a child's intellect without considering his emotional needs, he may use this defensively to protect himself emotionally. This can feel like an intellectual false-self which acts as a defense against dependency. On the other hand, functioning and educational achievement can strengthen a child's self-esteem, enabling him to feel less vulnerable to disintegration and more able to make use of a localized regression. Learning has the potential to facilitate emotional growth.

The way in which teachers work with children has the potential of both enabling academic achievement and providing appropriate relationship experiences. However, achieving these two aims may not feel easy and could seem to be in conflict. Teaching and learning does potentially involve dependency. First of all a child may be mistrustful and defended against the vulnerability involved in learning. Gradually through the relationship with his teacher, he may begin to trust her. As with other dependant relationships, he may feel that she has something good, which is not his and which he would like. If he can allow himself, the child may be able to take something from her, which helps him to learn. He may need to develop a belief in a benevolent teacher before he can learn academically.

Treatment is about providing opportunities for children to internalize valuable relationship experiences of which they have previously been deprived. It is not possible simply to transfer a child development model to our work with children. For example, while some of our children have the emotional needs of an infant, in other respects they are different and in some areas far more developed. Intellectual and emotional aspects of the mind are linked together but also separate.

If a child is able and capable of achievement but is held back, this could be very frustrating for him and could be detrimental to his development, for instance, by feeding into his low self-esteem and sense of being no good. A child needs the opportunity to work at a level he is capable of, emotionally, cognitively and intellectually. For instance, if a child has a high IQ, that may not mean he is ready for demanding educational work. Too much pressure can cause emotional and educational progress to be set back. Careful judgments need to be made about a child's capacity to make use of 'failing'. Failing as well as succeeding can be of value but only if the experience can be made sense of by the child.

The approach towards education is based on the individual. Each child has an individual education plan, which is aimed at meeting his own needs within the framework of the National Curriculum. For example, children studying for GCSEs are worked with in a way that acknowledges their emotional needs. There is the opportunity for regressed play in school. If there is going to be more structure there will be less room for spontaneous play. This drew our attention to the importance of play and we wondered if there is enough room for this in the home.

We noted that home and school are becoming more distinct in their tasks, which implies a greater degree of separation between the two. As long as the child can make sense of the differences and adults are also clear about them, this can be a benefit to a child's treatment and development. It is important for adults to think about their own anxieties related to this issue, such as their own experiences and feelings connected to: school and education; rivalry between school and home; achieving and not achieving. If these anxieties can be thought about, they are less likely to impinge in an unhelpful way.

Though the National Curriculum can be used in a way that is appropriate to children at all different levels, its use will raise expectations to do with achievement. Increasing pressure is likely to be put onto the education department, possibly from social workers, parents and education authorities to demonstrate that each child is receiving the appropriate education. Careful work is necessary to ensure each child's needs are at the centre of his treatment and education plan. The children's treatment can be understood to consist of therapeutic child care and therapeutic education.

It is arguable education has been undervalued in the past and is now asserting its identity. Children in the Community are achieving more from an educational point of view and are leaving better equipped in this respect. There could be, though, an anxiety that teachers are too identified with teaching and are not paying enough attention to the child's emotional stage of development.

The next section considers to what extent the children's care and education both need to be part of the same theoretical framework.

The importance of education in the treatment of traumatized children

This discussion, which forms the basis for this section, took place not long after the Cotswold Community was taken over by NCH. This change would mean being registered as a school rather than a CHE (community home with education). Inevitably, this change created some anxiety and prompted us to look at the implications and review the task of education. The education of traumatized children is an important and complex issue and relevant to those involved in therapeutic work and education with these children. Before exploring this, it is necessary to provide a context.

In 1997 the Community had provisional registration as a school. A process took place with NCH to decide the appropriate registration. With a school, the emphasis is on education and with a CHE it is more on the care side. This emphasis is reinforced by the inspection process. The primary inspection of a school is carried out by Ofsted and of a CHE by the National Care Standards Commission. The main objective is to achieve a registration that is supportive of its primary task, the treatment of emotionally unintegrated children. Whatever the registration, education in the academic sense has been a growing concern for all those involved in residential child care. Young people leaving care are often less qualified than their peers and this is often cited as one of the reasons for further difficulties after care (DH/DfEE 2000).

Until recent years, the approach to education in the Community was largely focused on the provision of a facilitating space in which children could learn through play and exploration. Education time was largely unstructured and an environment was provided in which children were supported in learning at their own pace. As a child evolved in his learning, education staff would be alert to this and provide him with further educational opportunities. For many years, children have been provided with structured individual reading times. However, these times were also linked to the idea of primary provision, a bit like a parent reading to an infant or vice versa.

One of the treatment aims has been to take the pressure off children to behave or perform at a chronological age level. This pressure could lead to a defensive type of functioning where the child will not allow himself to regress. At the same time, the therapeutic approach has also been to support the child's ability to function or to provide ego-functioning (Dockar-Drysdale 1990d, p.157). Some children feel less threatened by regression if their sense of self-esteem is built up in other areas. It has become clear that unintegrated children can be capable of academic achievement. Emotional and academic learning do not necessarily go hand in hand.

The approach of the school has become increasingly structured. This has been to ensure that the National Curriculum is provided to meet each child's individual needs. The National Curriculum is applied in a way that still enables children to have a regressed type of early childhood experience through play. The approach is largely about getting alongside a child and helping him to learn by adapting to his need. This adaptability happens within an expectation that each child will be working on a particular subject at a set time in each day. Mostly it feels as though each child's educational development is going in tandem with his emotional development. Generally, education and care staff work jointly together to help each child develop.

Sometimes a child's progress in school is the most tangible way he can measure his development. There is a step-by-step aspect about it and each step can boost his sense of self-worth and value. Conversely, there is a danger of implying to a child that he is unable to learn because of his emotional problems. A child's anxieties and worries about learning are now faced more directly in school, rather than waiting for them to emerge.

The main reason for these developments is to ensure that each child is offered the best educational opportunities possible. This provision includes meeting the external requirements connected to education. However, the emphasis on provision is different to an emphasis on outcomes. In the present education climate it is easy to be drawn into an overemphasis on outcomes measured through examination results. Teaching can aim at the exam rather than the child. Our therapeutic approach is about providing a facilitating environment, where each child can develop in his own way in his own time. We are trying to help him become a learner in the full sense of the word.

Rather than academic progress being spread over the normal school years, it is bunched together more for children here. Children who are at the beginning of their learning may feel a huge distance from children taking exams. It is important that we try to protect children at different stages from feeling a pressure to move on before they are ready. We need to give equal attention to all of the achievements a child makes, including his struggles where we feel his progress is very slow. We should not preempt his development. We need to be careful not to judge children purely in terms of examination results.

The therapeutic approach, which includes both care and education, first enables a child to reach and acknowledge a feeling of not knowing and of vulnerability. He may then allow himself to be dependant and believe in the idea of a benign teacher-carer who has something good, which she wants to give him to enrich his life.

The child's experience of separation between care and education

In addition to education, going to school provides children with an experience of emotional and physical separation that is a normal key aspect of child development. For traumatized children this separation may not have been achieved and their emotional difficulties can make this a complex and challenging task. The anxieties usually experienced in infancy and the first school years may still be prevalent and need to be worked through. This discussion is relevant to the education experience of traumatized children and in particular where residential care and education are provided on the same site.

The model that we have been moving towards is one of clearer distinction between the tasks of care and education, but which maintains the shared task of facilitating the growth and development of children. This is a shift from a model where children received education within a distinct unit incorporating home and school, to one where children leave their home to go to school. The difference may be one of degree, though there is now a greater emphasis on the experience of separation. All children with whom we work, except the most emotionally unintegrated, have some capacity to experience separation and differentiation. Children who have no such capacity would need an intense level of individual provision before being ready for school.

As work with unintegrated children is centered on facilitating dependant attachments, it can be difficult at the same time to manage and support separation. Children and their carers may have powerfully ambivalent and anxious feelings about separation. The potential danger is that we fail to stick with feelings such as guilt and rejection, and deny separation to make these feelings more bearable. For example, a carer may communicate to teachers in such a way that it implies a child is not ready or capable to sustain any separation. This could result in an overemphasis on the need for teachers to know everything about the child, so that they can more or less treat him as if they were his carer. Any breakdown for the child in school could then be seen as a failure by the teacher to understand him, leading to an even greater concern that communication is improved. The child may pick up a feeling that he cannot manage the separation and needs to be with his carer. This could result in him frequently needing to return to the house.

As the way in which care and education work together has changed, the structures and routines between the two have not necessarily been adapted in a way to reflect the changes. Different approaches to house–school handovers have developed without being clear how they relate to the task.

In all the primary houses, the teachers go to the house before school starts. The teachers read the daily log and join the house meeting. Information is passed on about the school day and children ask questions. In some cases, children ask if they can take various items to school. As the teachers have a lot of information about what is happening in the house, a child who is beginning to have a sense of separation could feel there is not enough room to differentiate his behavior between house and school. For example, if he has had a difficulty with his carer, he may wish to arrive in school and present a different mood. Additionally, it could be more difficult for children to express difficult feelings about school and leave these in the house if this is going to be witnessed by the teachers. If the teachers see him as he was in the house, they may feel to him as if they are an extension of the house staff. While this could feel reassuring at times, it may not encourage the child to recognize his own anxieties and find his own ways of coping with them outside of his primary attachment. While all adults who work with him should show sensitivity to his feelings, there should also be a difference in the ways different people know and work with him.

GCSEs and the relationship between a child's academic and emotional development

During the 1990s the number of children taking GCSEs and the number of GCSEs taken by each child began to increase significantly. This had an impact on the culture of the Community and the related matters that needed to be understood.

Children in the Community tend to begin working towards a GCSE exam when they are assessed as capable of meeting the demands involved. This tends to be based more on their overall development, rather than on chronological age. In mainstream school children begin taking GCSE subjects at about 14 years of age and sit the exams two years later. Occasionally some exams are taken a year earlier. A child in the Community may begin a GCSE earlier than this, or in some cases start later and complete the subject in one rather than two years. An advantage of taking the GCSEs spread out can be to reduce the pressure of studying for many examinations at the same time. However, we need to be careful not to push children too early. If the pressure is too great, this can disrupt development. If there is a possibility of failure, this needs to be an experience he can learn from and move on. There is also the risk of holding children back, sometimes through a fear of failure or success or an overprotectiveness. The process of an individual learning will also lead to changes in the relationships between him and others. If these potential changes are not thought about and acknowledged the anxieties involved could get in the way of and block emotional growth and learning.

To what extent can the education we provide be led by children's needs rather than other constraints? For example, can we run lessons where some children in the group are working towards an examination while others are not? Can we only value learning and studying a subject at a certain level if it is leading towards a qualification? There is an increasing emphasis on educational attainment, which can lead to a huge pressure on children to pass and achieve. How can we support a child at the stage that he has reached, without always thinking where we want him to get to?

To fail in an attainment-led culture can feel particularly awful to children who have low self-esteem. Our aim is that we help children with these feelings, while also working in such a way that we pay attention to and celebrate achievements. We need to be careful that we do not lose our own focus on what is achievement and development for a child. The emphasis on GCSE-type attainment may mean that we focus less on the broader skills a child can develop from the general living process and opportunities this can create. For instance, in the past many children at the Community have developed interests in things such as carpentry, electrics and farming. For some children these interests have then developed into work opportunities. There is a danger that we devalue some of these interests if they do not fit neatly into the educational system. As the education task becomes more distinct, how can we continue to offer children education in the widest sense of the word and not just in terms of the National Curriculum?

It is essential that education and care staff communicate well and work together on these matters. There are a number of possible scenarios in this area of work: we misunderstand a child's needs and work with him in such a way that increases his anxiety and difficulties; his needs are understood but not by all the adults who work with him; misunderstandings, conflict and suspicion between adults is picked up by the child and is distracting to him; there is a shared approach to work with the child, which he complies with by offering a picture of himself which is not true; there is a shared approach, which enables emotional and educational development to run side by side and complement each other.

Care and education staff need to have a joint understanding of a child's treatment that is based on his needs. To some extent, this understanding will develop through a process of exploration, explanation and negotiation.

Regression within the education setting

The approach developed by Dockar-Drysdale centered on the concept of regression and primary provision. Children were sometimes supported in a regressed state in school. With the shift to a more educational approach, we wondered whether regression ought to be more localized within the home and school more based upon age-appropriate expectations. Some children have suffered such developmental delay due to their extreme deprivation and abuse that they are not so much regressing as having never moved forward. These children really do need a basic level of primary experience in all aspects of their environment before they can move on. This experience provides the foundation for development. The Community conceived the idea that a foundation group in the school would be necessary to meet the needs of these children. This group would provide early educational experience within a highly supportive environment. Having broadly agreed with the task of the foundation group we examined the issue of regression in more detail.

The assessment during a child's referral will need to cover his educational needs in detail so this can be included alongside the assessment of his emotional needs. The issue of regression is particularly relevant to this group of children. There will be some emotionally unintegrated (frozen) children (Dockar-Drysdale 1958), whose development is so impaired that their treatment is less about moving forward from where they are and starting at the beginning. They have not progressed to a point from which they can regress. A child who regresses must have internalized some primary experiences and evolved to a point from which he can go back.

For children who do need to regress our general aim is to try to localize this as much as possible within a specific dependant attachment. An environment is provided that allows that to happen with a focus on the need for primary provision within this relationship. Hence the term 'focal-carer'. However, we cannot predict exactly how or to what extent a child will regress. For some children the regression largely takes place within this context and outside of it he functions at a chronologically age-appropriate level. For others the regression is localized within the house as a whole and not confined to just the focal-carer relationship. Sometimes a child may need to regress completely for a short period of time.

It seems right that school does not encourage regression, though there needs to be some receptivity to the possibility of it. For example, a child who is regressed may actually go backwards in terms of his educational ability. We have seen cases where a child has temporarily lost the ability to read, as his need to be provided for has been so great. At these times, it is helpful to be accepting rather than critical of the child. Clarity about the reasons for these situations is necessary.

It is not appropriate for a focal-carer role to be provided within the school. However, a high level of care is needed at times, in the same way playgroup workers provide for the emotional and physical needs of infants in their parents' absence. As the playgroup worker or teacher in this situation is likely to be one of the first adult figures for the child other than his parents, it is likely the child will perceive the worker or teacher as a parental figure. The issue for the worker to remember is the distinction between being in this role and actually being the parent. As this is likely to be one of the earliest separations for the child he may not find it easy to make these distinctions. A good level of communication between the adults involved is necessary to ensure the child's needs are met without blurring boundaries and roles.

One of the needs of children in the foundation group will be the need for food. This need is likely to be greater than with children who are further on in their development. Holding on to experiences and waiting is not easy for children in this group. Feeling hungry is not easy to tolerate and the concept of time before the next meal may not mean much to these children. Some kind of provision needs to be available in a way that meets this need, but provided in a way that is not too distracting. Thinking about provision for individual need will be required as well as general provision for the group. Thinking and discussion will need to go on between the children's carer (or carers) and teacher, to find the best way for meeting these needs.

House–school handovers

So far as education is concerned, it does not seem necessary for teachers to go to the house for the handover. It is possible for grown-ups in the house to prepare children for school and pass on significant information about the day. The smaller detail about the school day can be explained when children arrive in school. Teachers could phone over to the house for a handover before children go over to school. Given the difficulties we work with, there is a need for teachers to have certain information before the school day begins so that this can be thought about and any plans made. This information should include matters about child protection, medical concerns, significant difficulties between particular children, absences of any children from the school day, significant events for particular children (for example, the visit of a parent).

When children are brought over to school, there is likely to be some anxiety between carers and teachers about the handover. When children are collected from school, teachers will need to give a brief handover to an adult from each house group about any particular event or incident. Handovers should be clear and focused, and we should be careful that they do not get used as a way of off-loading anxiety between the house and school.

The working relationship and rapport between a carer and teacher is critical in helping a child feel contained by their shared concern for his development, while also recognizing their different roles. There is an informal aspect to handovers, which is about establishing and maintaining this rapport. The safety and containment of children in the house and school will be affected by both the clarity of communication as well as underlying feelings between the two. To improve the relationship between care staff and teachers one education team has set up a link person system. One of the team is allocated to each house as a link person, with the aim of developing a closer relationship between the house and school.

The involvement of a child's carer with his time in school

In a setting where home and school are provided on site, the relationship between the two is close and establishing how close it should be is continuing work. The aim is to ensure that home and school staff work positively together enabling the child to experience care and education as being integrated as well as separate and distinct. Careful consideration of the issues and clear boundaries are necessary to ensure that care and education can function alongside each other without the task of either becoming blurred or merged into the other.

In thinking about a child's time in school and how his carer can show an interest and be involved, it is necessary to consider both the importance of what the child does in school and the separation between the child and carer during this time. The carer's involvement must be appropriate concerning these two matters. There are a number of possible ways for a carer to be involved, for example:

- discussing the child's time in school with the teachers;
- taking the child to school and collecting him, giving enough time to look at his work;
- helping the child do homework in the house;

- generally talking with the child about school;
- spending regular planned time with the child in school.

It is not a good idea for a carer just to drop into school unexpectedly. This would not help with separation and could be quite distracting. The aim is to establish concern and interest in the child's time in school, so that the whole of the child's experience and development is being thought about. Once this is established, it will be necessary for the carer to reduce actual time in school to prevent confusion with primary provision that takes place in the house.

Working with breakdown in the school

The discussion on this topic took place following a demanding period of working with breakdown in the school. Significant difficulties were being experienced in the new education system and the changed relationships between school and houses. The matters raised in this section are again particularly relevant to settings where residential care and education are provided on the same site.

One of the underlying principles in the Community's structure is the idea of containing boundaries or membranes. For example, a focal-carer provides a containing boundary around a child. The carer and her preoccupation support the child's fragile ego. Where this fails or breaks down there will be additional containment provided by the house culture and team, such as the role of back-up person. The house boundary represented by the house manager provides another layer of potential containment. Where the house does not contain a child, there are further boundaries within the Community as a whole. In practice, the way this works is by providing a third person in a relationship, which can help create a thinking space. This in itself can help to change dynamics and contain anxieties and conflicts. There is always a senior manager available to houses, during evenings and weekends for this purpose. This person is clear about her supportive task. In the previous education system, the house-education team provided a similar sort of containment. The close working relationships allowed for a high level of sensitivity, understanding and support. Of course, there could be points of tension and breakdown between the two, requiring support from senior managers.

With the new education system there has been a reduction in closeness and sensitivity between house and education teams. It is not so easy to understand each other's context. For example, the daily handover meetings in the previous system between a teacher and house manager enabled a continuing relationship and understanding to develop. These points of contact also gave opportunities to refer to general matters and concerns. In many ways, the present structures do not offer the same degree of containment. The simple fact of knowing who will be coming up for the handover or who is available to talk to if there is a breakdown can be supportive. If this type of support is lacking then primitive feelings are likely to build up. Strong feelings and anxieties are evoked in work with children. Where there is a lack of communication and understanding between adults these feelings are more likely to be displaced or projected. A persecutory and blaming atmosphere can soon develop. For children to feel safe and held there needs to be a sense of trust between the child's teachers and carers.

While there are some losses involved in the change to the new education system, some aspects of working relationships remain the same. There are possibilities of adapting and developing new approaches. For example, we can develop containing relationships between a teacher and house team through continuing communication and understanding. Specific teachers taking on the role of link person for a specific house may help this. This is similar to a school model where parents relate mainly to one teacher, though the child is often taught by a number of teachers. This gives a sense of clarity which helps a supportive relationship to develop. To improve containment it seems necessary to clarify the process for working with breakdown and who is available to the school from houses as a point of contact. To provide the most effective support we also need to find a way of achieving an overview of the school day across the whole group of children.

To some extent, the changes will take time to work through while new relationships between teachers and children, teachers and teachers, and teachers and carers grow and develop. There are many new relationships to be established. The relationship between teacher and child is central to the child's learning. With the changes to and development of the education task, the emphasis in work between a teacher and child will be less focused on the relationship. For example, a child who is disruptive in school is more often worked with by an adult coming in, enabling the teacher to continue teaching. The option of the supporting adult working with the group while the teacher works something through with the individual child has not been used so much. Comments such as that the supporting adult cannot teach the group may be used to rationalize this. The supporting adult can, however, oversee the group's work as set by the teacher. The teacher often follows work through with the child later in the house or school. The way in which disruption is responded to and worked through needs careful thought, so that appropriate authority and containment between teacher and child can develop. Flexibility should be maintained in our options for working on these matters.

Learning support

From the beginning of the Cotswold Community, all children living together in one house would attend the same education area (poly) together as a group. The staff from the house would provide direct support to their poly group. As the education moved towards a school approach with groups based more upon educational key stages, the single house-poly unit no longer existed, so the responsibility for support became less clear and at the same time the separation of house and school became more distinct and necessary. The concept of learning support provided by the school emerged during this period. This is a useful model in any education setting where children struggle to sustain uninterrupted time in the setting.

The main aim of the learning support resource would be to provide an additional layer of support for children between the school and house. Children who are struggling could be worked with either within their own classroom or within a specific learning support area. Symbolically this helps to create the sense of a school area that is more than a group of classrooms. Previously there has been little or no sense of school space between the class or school and the house. The closest to it has been the opportunity on a few occasions for a child to spend time in another class.

Matters for consideration

The actual operation of the learning support resource could be complex. If the emphasis of their work is mainly on anticipation and prevention of breakdown, the resource could become absorbed directly into the classrooms, like an extra resource to increase teacher-to-child ratios. The risk could be that this increases reliance on the resource and reduces expectations on children to function. If the resource becomes too easily absorbed, there would be little capacity to respond to further breakdown. On the other hand, if the resource is only used when things have completely broken down it may feel more like a crisis intervention resource. The potential emphasis on physical interventions at these points could create an unhelpful picture of the resource for children and adults.

The availability of a distinct space for the resource within the school does seem appropriate. A clear sense of a boundary between the resource and the classrooms will be necessary. The management of this boundary will need to strike a balance between anticipatory support and crisis intervention. The question as to when to involve additional staff from the house will need careful analysis. Communication, boundary management and authority need to be clear for the learning support resource to work with the potential difficulties involved.

The role of care staff within the school also needs careful planning. The roles of education and care staff have become more separate and distinct. This has largely centered around teachers becoming less involved in care and house tasks and focused increasingly on education (previously teachers worked in the houses some evenings and weekends). These changes sometimes raise anxieties and concerns about splits developing between care and education. The separation of education and care in itself will not create splits as long as the relationship between the two is seen as the essential part of the whole. It could be argued that clarity in role and task is likely to reduce splitting.

If care staff are in the role of learning support resource and become directly involved in classrooms, this could cause some difficulties for children in separating from their carers and focusing on education. There could be confusion about a carer also being a teacher. The aim is to support each child's capacity to function within the school. This also encourages primary provision to be localized within house-based carer relationships. Roles could become blurred if the learning support resource becomes too involved with children's education, rather than on support by establishing a sense of boundary between school and house.

The involvement and interest of carers in their children's education is positive and supportive. At times, it can feel as if this interest slips. For example, when work in the house is very stressful, a carer might be relieved to drop children off at school. The school may feel more like it is providing a childminding function rather than education. This can also happen the other way round: where teachers are so relieved to reach the end of the day that little space is left for considering what goes on outside of school. Systems need establishing to ensure there is a strong sense of connection between teachers and carers.

The issue of breakdown is particularly significant now. Anxieties about change and, in particular, mixing children from different houses together in the school, raise concerns about potential breakdown and acting out by children. The learning support concept could lend itself as a focus for these anxieties both from education and care, as it bridges between the two. For some of the reasons discussed above and for other practical ones, it might not be clear what the best model is. The nature of what is provided within the school, the positive support of care teams and communication between the two are essential components of helping the changes to work. We have our own anxieties about all these things and could displace them onto the children by, for example, saying the children will not cope – and then onto the learning support resource as a container for children's acting out.

School homework

The issue of school homework highlights the difficulty for emotionally troubled children in achieving educationally and the conflict that can be felt in those caring for them between addressing emotional and educational needs. A child with severe emotional problems needs specialized help to treat his emotional difficulties. This is hard work requiring time and energy. A child in this situation needs time for relaxation and an opportunity to be relieved of pressure.

Now there is a greater sense of school within the Community it seems some children are expecting more of a mainstream school experience and have begun to ask for homework. Homework needs thinking about. The implications need to be considered carefully by all the adults working with a child. The Community's structure is not entirely comparable to a school-family situation. Children are placed here for treatment that includes care and education. The work involved for children takes place in the house and school. In the house, each child is expected to be involved with group meetings, individual meetings, work on his feelings, communication and primary provision. This is inevitably an intense experience and partly why it is so important for children to have an outside family placement for breaks away.

If a child is asking for homework, the teacher should find out why. We need to think what underlying factors might be connected to a child's request. It could be a reflection of his wish to continue learning. If this is coming from him, he could be supported in practicing what he has learnt and talking with his carer. This has also to be done within the context of working with all of his needs. The child may be anxious about other things and is using the homework to avoid them. Similarly, adults could also wish to avoid something in this way. Homework can be used in a way that controls the use of time. Sometimes a child's anxiety about endings and completing things he is doing make it difficult for him to leave unfinished work in the school. The main aim in work with him at these times should be to help him with this anxiety. We could try to plan his work so he is able to complete it within the school time or help him with the feelings he has about leaving something unfinished. This may also be connected to how he feels about endings and transitions in the wider sense.

It is not helpful for emotionally unintegrated children to be set homework with the expectation that it must be completed. Obviously, with children who are approaching GCSEs there is a different level of expectation. On a practical level, thought needs to be given from both house and education teams, about what goes from house to school and vice versa. Treatment processes are carefully planned for children in both the house and school. The expectations about a child's time in house or school need to be set primarily by those adults working in the particular area. If anything is to cross over the house–school boundary, discussion and agreement between all the adults involved is necessary.

An adult's wish for a child to learn also needs thinking about. Is it based on a realistic understanding of his capability and needs? Is the adult anxious that he should learn to prove he has good carers and teachers? A child's carer and other adults who work with him should be attentive to his interest and curiosity in learning. This can happen in many different ways through the course of day-to-day living. Showing an interest in and supporting his schoolwork is part of this.

Education staff's involvement with needs assessments

As care and education became more separate the question arose of how a child's experience in school would be included as part of his needs assessment. Previously education staff attended a weekly team meeting with care staff. Needs assessments would be carried out in these meetings. The education staff's contribution into the meeting would not be possible on a regular basis so we needed to reconsider how they could contribute to needs assessment. In all settings working with traumatized children, the sharing of information between teachers and carers is essential in trying to gain an overall picture of a child's needs and development.

Now that teachers are not part of a specific house-education treatment team, they are no longer part of house team meetings. The care teams work on needs assessments and therapeutic management programs in these meetings (Dockar-Drysdale 1990d, pp.158, 164). Ideally, it would be most beneficial for all those adults who work directly with a specific child to be involved in a joint team discussion. If this is not possible or practical, there are different ways of ensuring all aspects of a child are brought together. His treatment plan will be based on an understanding of this whole picture. It is a particularly important part of treatment that the adults working with a child are able to put their different experiences together and bear this in mind.

There will be many opportunities, formal and informal, for carers and teachers to share their experiences of children. There will be regular daily handovers. Focal-carers and teachers will meet at the beginning and end of each term to discuss each of the focal-carer's children. As well as focusing on academic educational progress, a significant part of the communication will be about a child's relationships with teachers and children, attitude towards others and the development of the capacity for concern. All of this communication between care and education staff needs to be borne in mind and included in the work on needs assessments and therapeutic management programs. In addition to this, an education team could write something to be included or on occasions a teacher who is particularly involved with the child could join the meeting. Completed assessments and programs will be given and shared with the relevant education team, which gives another opportunity for feedback to ensure all relevant aspects of each child are considered.

Working on conflict between care and education staff

The task of providing effectively integrated care and education for emotionally troubled young people is inherently challenging. Providing either one is difficult; providing both and managing the relationship can be exceptionally difficult. Young people's experience of home and school, the relationship between the two, and more general issues such as separation and rivalry are raised. The staff involved in care and education will become a collective container for such matters and will be challenged to make sense of what they are containing. They will do this while considering their own questions related to real objective differences between care and education, their feelings about these differences, as well as their personal and subjective feelings related to their own experiences of care and education. At a time in the Community's history when the status of care and education was fundamentally changing due to the change in registration from CHE to school, matters that often arose were experienced more intensely. The capacity of care and education staff to contain the feelings involved was tested to the limit. We felt it useful to have a series of discussions, whereby the issues manifesting themselves in the staff group could be thought about and understood.

There is envy of the education team by care staff which often focused on the perception that education staff have more flexible and better hours of work. There is also a feeling that both the work of the education staff and their time off are more protected. One perception is that care staff are interrupted more often when they are doing things without children, that is, to respond to school breakdowns. There is envy from education staff towards the special relationship they perceive care staff to have with children. Some care staff acknowledge that they would not like to lose the relationship they have with children and feel protective of this. The resentment and envy may be greater during periods of change. At these times difficult feelings, which are not acknowledged and understood, might be disowned and projected onto another group. The other group becomes the 'enemy within'. Sometimes these feelings are expressed indirectly, such as joking about the 'easy' time education staff have.

It is one of the treatment aims to provide an opportunity for children to experience separation from their primary care. In this sense, the school should be in its own distinct area and the education staff a bit removed from the house. One of the difficulties was to provide for a whole range of needs in the same place. For instance, different children have needs that are similar to the needs of children at the stages of: mother and toddler group; preschool nursery or playgroup; and primary school reception class. The task of care staff in relation to the school is often to be available to children in a 'maternal' sense. The staff holding this responsibility can expect to feel as though they are constantly on call in the same way parents with an infant would.

Care staff can support children's education in different ways. Whenever possible it is a positive aim to try to support the school situation so that the children's functioning can be maintained and restored. At times, there can be a feeling of competition and suspicion between care and education staff. These feelings often centre on matters like: 'This child is not ready for school, why are you bringing him?' or 'Why are you sending him back to the house? You should be able to manage this.'

Sometimes resentment, envy and jealousy become focused on matters connected with money. For instance, care staff express feelings about teachers being paid more. This area of conflict could possibly be a displacement of general feelings and anxieties related to money and the work we do. Children often bring this to our attention with questions about how much we are paid, and comments like 'you only do this for the money, you don't really care.'

Chapter 5

Play

Play is central to child development and has been used throughout the Cotswold Community's history as a key part of the therapeutic approach. Winnicott (1971) developed a theoretical understanding of human nature that emphasized the importance of play and creativity in emotional development. Dockar-Drysdale (1963a) used this in her work and expanded upon symbolic communication in the treatment of emotionally disturbed children. If we are aware of the importance of play and value it, there are great opportunities for facilitating play in all aspects of work with traumatized children.

Opportunities for play in houses

Do children have enough opportunity to play freely or spontaneously in houses? This concern has partly come about through a sense that school is becoming more structured and because of the emphasis on planned activity in houses. The emphasis on planned activity is connected to the assumption that emotionally unintegrated children are not able to play freely, so we organize things to try to prevent a collapse into chaos. During infancy, a child needs someone to be with him while he tries things out, to make it safe and help him with the anxieties involved. Through her playful involvement with the infant, the adult reflects the infant's play back to him. This helps to hold the situation, enabling the infant to sustain, enjoy and make sense of his experience. Gradually through internalizing this experience, the infant is then able to play alone in the presence of another.

Play is valuable in development because it encourages:

- exploration
- stimulation
- imagination
- creativity
- tactile experience
- working through of emotional experience.

There are various ways in which this can be encouraged:

- Have plenty of toys around – bath toys, puppets, old clothes for dressing up, paint, glue.
- Allow objects to be used playfully. Young children often play well with things they find laying around and then use imaginatively.
- Try not to get too anxious about toys and materials becoming muddled or a few things being damaged. The muddle can be put back into order.
- Create spaces that are not filled with planned activity. Adults and children could just 'be' together or maybe the adult could get on with some 'house job' while a child plays close by.
- Even planned activity can leave room for spontaneity and does not have to follow a rigid pattern. For example, different kinds of play may emerge during a walk if space is made for it.
- The team should work closely together in this area, ensuring play is a central focus in the house.

Play and activity with children

Play, in the sense of imaginative and creative games, inevitably has uncertainty involved in it – what will happen, how and when will it end? On the other hand, structured games and activities are more predictable and certain in their outcome. While there are benefits to structured activity, it can also be used defensively as a way of avoiding the anxieties in facilitating play. Those involved in work with traumatized children have a key task of enabling play and, to achieve this, careful thought and attention are necessary.

Play is central to healthy child development. Given the deprivation the children we work with have suffered, it is essential that there are opportunities for play. Rather than discuss the reasons why play is valuable, we shall discuss some of the difficulties we experience in facilitating play. At times, it seems as if there is not much room for spontaneous play. The following difficulties can contribute to this.

A lack of resources can make it difficult to respond to a child's wish to play and explore. For example, there are times of the day when staff are stretched, so these times are often tightly managed with little room for spontaneity. If this is the case, we need to be careful not to let this slip into a predominant culture of responding negatively to children's requests. High levels of anxiety and stress can make it difficult for adults and children to feel playful. Responses to children's wishes may be overreactive and controlling. If adults are receiving powerful negative feelings from children, this can stir up punitive-type feelings by way of response.

The general balance between structured and unstructured play could shift too far towards structure. This may also be connected with anxieties about control and safety. There might be a fear of what will happen in an unstructured space. Structured activities such as watching the television, playing video games, tag and football can be used defensively to have a break and emotionally switch off. It can feel necessary from time to time to switch off a bit and do something that is fairly predictable, structured and 'safe'.

The children's anxiety and vulnerability in relation to play could be projected or displaced onto the adults so that obstacles are put in the way of play. This may also happen the other way round. Adults might feel envious of a child's capacity to play freely and if this is not acknowledged then adults may not be so encouraging of play.

We should question and monitor continually whether we are facilitating and actively promoting opportunities for play. Because children are likely to find this difficult, we need to provide an interesting and stimulating environment, as well as supporting gestures or initiatives coming from children. A lot of thought should go into what adults are providing. Partly for the reasons listed above, it is easy to slip into the habit of always providing the same sort of activity. This can help to keep children occupied but may not require much emotional investment.

As long as the balance seems right between structured games and play, the reality that it is not possible to play freely all the time also has its positive side. Many different skills and interests can be developed and encouraged through structured activity. The expectation on a child to relate to the reality of living in a group provides a balance to the experience where he feels the world evolves around him and his wishes. Sometimes he will be able to play what he wants and at other times he will have to join in with others. This helps him to develop a sense of boundary between internal and external reality. Children might respond angrily to this as if we are depriving them. This can evoke the feeling that our provision is not good enough, that we are too harsh and do not care. If we consider these feelings and try to distinguish the reality, it is possible to say no while still acknowledging the child's wish in a supportive way.

Children playing games that have an element of danger

Taking risks and experiencing degrees of danger can be a valuable aspect of play. Providing this experience in a way that is also safe is a difficult challenge in ordinary parenting and especially in work with emotionally traumatized children and young people.

Do we provide appropriate opportunity for children to stretch themselves and find their limits by playing games with an element of danger in them? An activity such as climbing is an example. These types of activity or game can enable a child to explore his limits, to experience feelings of excitement and anxiety, and to manage those feelings successfully. The principle applies to all children, though the level of appropriate risk will depend upon the child's emotional stage of development.

Traumatized children might act out their frightening and dangerous experiences through play. The acting out could be an attempt to resolve their trauma by working through it. Children who have experienced high levels of anxiety and danger can also become drawn to the feeling of excitement and fear. The main therapeutic task with emotionally unintegrated children is to provide an environment where a child can experience the primary provision he has substantially missed so far in his life. Part of this includes providing an environment where he will literally be physically safe and protected from anxieties that feel unsafe and overwhelming to him. This requires a level of supervision and preoccupation from the adults similar to that which an infant aged up to two years would ideally experience. Having had this experience, an infant can hopefully gain a sense of being safe and thought about, which enables him to explore the world gradually with some confidence.

As children develop emotionally, they will be ready to experience a less closely supervised environment. However, these children are still at an early developmental stage and careful thought needs to go into what kind of activity or situations are appropriate for them to cope with. It is not always easy to make rules about what is safe and what is not. Besides the clear cases of what is not safe, we have to assess risk, taking into consideration an individual child's needs, the group's needs and the adult's anxieties. If a child asks an adult to join in play that she feels uncomfortable with, feels the game is not safe or causes too much anxiety, it is probably better to explain that to the child rather than to join in with him. It is possible to say: 'I don't feel like playing this game because…' Sometimes there could be a lack of anxiety for adults about children playing dangerous games or being unsupervised. One of the things to consider is whether this reflects an underlying aggression from the adults towards the children.

The type of toys or games a child is allowed to have in the house should depend upon what it represents to him as well as the anxieties it raises for the group of children. One way of finding this out is observing what toys children bring back or reject. For instance, in some groups children have not been allowed to have sticks because of the anxieties raised for other children by associations and memories of being beaten.

The symbolic and reality-based use of toys in children's play

Children will often play with toys that can have both a meaning that is relevant in the real world and one that is more symbolically related to the child's internal fantasy world. We might feel unsure whether we respond to the external or internal meaning of the play, or both. This can be especially so when the external meaning seems to be in conflict with our own values.

For example, children may play cowboys and Indians, and use this play to symbolically represent conflict between good and bad, persecutor and victim. This play could be an integral process in the child's struggle towards holding ambivalent feelings, rather than splitting them. There might be many issues represented in this play such as aggression, concern, territory, boundaries and identity. However, there may be a difficulty for us in how we respond to the play, if it also actually represents cultural stereotypes or reinforces them. For example, the cowboys are good and civilized while Native Americans are bad and savage. This issue can arise about many different types of play and toys. It could be felt clearly in school, where there is an emphasis on education through play.

We concluded that it might be helpful for a child to play games that externalize conflicts to do with 'good' and 'bad' and for us not to give him the sense that his play is bad or wrong. If his play is creating or reinforcing actual stereotypes that he believes to be real, it may help to make a comment to him, regarding actual history or reality. For example, it could be helpful to describe something of day-to-day Native American culture if the child believes all 'Indians' are savages.

To provide a child with the opportunity to think of different possibilities and ways of using toys, it is helpful to have a wide range available. For example, if the child's Native Americans have other utensils and tools, as well as guns, arrows and spears, it gives the child more options in the way he uses and thinks about them. While we have used the example of 'Indians', the same issues apply to any group of people that children are using in this way.

The use of sensory experience rooms for children with learning difficulties

These rooms are designed without any hard edges and with padded walls so that children can throw themselves about without getting hurt. The room has cushions and would have music, lighting and textured objects specifically designed to stimulate the senses. Children using these rooms often start by letting off steam then calming down and getting in touch with their senses through focusing on some aspect of the room. The phrase 'coming to your senses' comes to mind, discovering one's self through the senses.

This led us on to thinking about different types of creative arts therapy such as music, art and drama therapy. These therapies and sensory room could be seen as something to add specifically to our culture. Alternatively, the value of these experiences could be incorporated and developed more in our day-to-day life. For instance, do we make enough of opportunities for different sensory experiences? How much thought do we put into the way we develop our physical environment? Do we enable children to enjoy sensory experiences such as eating and bathing? We could use music more in houses. Music and instruments can be used for communication as well as for learning how to play music. Musical instruments are useful to include alongside toys and other materials for children's meetings. A child could potentially use the instrument in many different ways.

Chapter 6

Therapeutic Communication – Individual and Group Meetings for Children

Communication with traumatized children is a major aspect of the therapeutic approach. Communication can happen one to one and in a group. These two aspects of communication can be used in different ways to meet different needs.

The use of individual meetings in the treatment of emotionally deprived children

The Cotswold Community developed individual meetings for therapeutic communication with children, with one of the carers in the child's house. This became a consistent part of the child's treatment. This chapter describes these meetings. The approach can be adapted in a wide range of settings where work with traumatized children is taking place.

Introduction

The aim of this chapter is to clarify the purpose of children's individual meetings with adults and establish some clear guidelines for the structure of those meetings. The adult meeting the child will normally be a member of the care staff working in the house the child lives in.

Purpose of the meeting

The main purpose of the meeting is to establish a safe, reliable space where an adult is actively available to receive communication, both conscious and unconscious, from the child. This communication can then be contained by the adult who is able to hold onto it and think about it, consciously and unconsciously. This is similar to the function of the mother in containing and making sense of an infant's intolerable feelings (Bion 1962). Gradually, as well as receiving back his own feelings in a more tolerable form, the infant is also able to internalize this capacity of the mother's and begin to manage more of his own feelings and think about them. Unfortunately, the children whom we work with have not experienced this to a 'good enough' degree, and are often overwhelmed by feelings that are felt to be intolerable and confusing. These children have a great need for us to provide this function for them and meetings are a focused way of making that provision.

It is necessary to examine what is needed to facilitate this purpose. We shall briefly outline the key aspects that enable the meeting to facilitate the child's communication, for it to be received and worked on.

The structure of the meeting

This includes who meets the child, when the meeting takes place, how long for, how often, and how the meeting is supported from outside.

Whoever meets a child will need to have emotional capacities as well as the physical time and space for the meeting. If a child is to begin to sense the possibility of an adult receiving his communication, the meetings need to be reliable. Unreliability is likely to confirm his experiences of there being no one available or able to contain his communication. The length and regularity of the meeting are factors in facilitating communication. The meetings need to be long enough for the child and adult to start the meeting, settle into it and end it. The meetings also need to be often enough for them to feel connected, with not too big a gap between them. Bearing these factors in mind, half an hour to one hour would seem to be an appropriate length of time. One meeting a week is probably the minimum in terms of regularity and two the maximum, with the more emotionally unintegrated children needing more frequent meetings. Some children may benefit from more than two meetings a week, though this might not be practical.

The meetings should be arranged during the time of the week when they are likely to be most reliable. To ensure the meeting is protected from disruption, the adult meeting the child should not be asked to do anything else during this time. If because of other commitments the adult is unable to meet the child, the child should be warned in advance and another time offered.

This at least gives the message that the meeting is taken seriously and acknowledges the adult's responsibility in missing the meeting. If the adult or child misses the meeting through illness, it is probably more appropriate to work on the feelings about that than to offer another time. If the child refuses to go to his meeting then this should be worked on with him by one of the adults in the house during the meeting time. This gives the message to the child and group of children that the house values meetings and shows concern for the child's difficulty. If the child is still unable to go to his meeting and misses it, then the child, the meeting adult, and another adult from the house should meet with the child at some other time to express their concern and deal with the difficulty. The adults in the house are taking on the parental responsibility in supporting the meeting. Another part of this role is in helping the child to attend his meeting regularly. One of the adults should remind the child of the time five minutes before the meeting is due to start and then help him to get to the meeting on time.

The role of the adult meeting the child

While the adult meeting the child is working within the structure already described, she must also provide part of the structure herself. If the child is to make good use of the meeting, it is essential that the adult continues in her role to receive his communication. For the child to feel safe enough to communicate he will need to test her capacity to do that. The beginning of the meetings provides the opportunity for the adult in establishing her role. During the first meeting, the adult should talk with the child about the meeting, explaining the purpose of it and giving the child an opportunity to ask questions. The meeting can be explained by saying something like: 'The meeting is a time for you, with an adult on your own, where you can say what you want to. You can say things in different ways, by talking, playing and drawing, or however you want as long as no one is physically hurt. The adult will not be asking you questions, except to help understand what you are saying.' The details about the time of the meeting and the meeting being protected from disruption should also be explained.

During the meeting, the adult has a number of responsibilities that help her to make her role evident. The adult should be in the room ready to start the meeting on time and not become involved in bringing the child to the meeting. This keeps the adult being available and not getting into any difficulties with the child, which could then make it difficult for a child to communicate to her or for her to receive the communication. As well as the adult being ready in the room at the start, all of the toys or objects to be used in the meeting should also be there. Once the child arrives for the meeting, the door should be closed and the adult manage the meeting within the room.

The adult has the role of holding and containing the child's communication and she will need to feel she can safely work with this during the meeting. She will need to put clear boundaries around the way the child is communicating to maintain safety. If the meeting does feel unsafe, with there being actual risk of injury to the child, adult or serious damage to the room, it could be necessary for the adult to stop the meeting and seek assistance to make things safe. If the adult is clear about this, then it is more likely the child will feel safe and be able to communicate his destructive, aggressive or confused feelings through talking, playing or drawing.

As well as appropriately containing the meeting as described above, the adult also needs to manage carefully the use of the meeting. For instance, the child might ask the adult to provide him with food during the meeting. While this may seem okay, it could have significant implications for the use of the meeting. If the adult provides food, the child could feel he is being given something good and seek reassurance in that rather than communicate difficult feelings. The food, literally and symbolically, may represent taking things in and keeping things down rather than letting them out. The food might be quite distracting for the child, in the sense of what does it taste like, look like and remind him of. The provision of food could also have associations for the child, which confuse his relationship with the adult. Food is connected strongly with primary provision and relationship with his carer, which could confuse the nature of provision in the meeting.

As the adult meeting the child most likely also works in his house, it is especially necessary that the adult distinguish between her roles in and out of the meeting. This distinction is too difficult to make if the adult meeting the child is also the one looking after him (in terms of primary provision) outside of the meeting. Whatever the adult's preoccupations are with the child outside of the meeting, these need to be prevented from impinging upon the meeting. If the adult were to use the meeting to talk over her concerns about the child or open up different concerns with him, he would not have the sense of someone being there primarily for him and his communication. Responding to the lead of the child whenever possible will help to create a sense of receptivity. It may not be necessary to say or do very much, just to be keenly observant and alert to the child. If the adult asks questions to clarify the child's communication, this will create links and connections and can be internalized by him as being thought of by someone. On the other hand, if the adult asks questions that are not to do with his communication, he might experience this as the adult being unable to think about him. If the child asks the adult to join in with his play, similarly she should respond to the child's play rather than bring in her own play. Obviously, this is not always easy to get right but if the adult is keenly focused on the child, he will be able to communicate whether he has been understood or not.

Having looked at the beginning and middle of the meeting, we shall now look at its ending. The ending of the meeting is important and potentially difficult as it is about completing an experience. The child's previous experience of endings may have been that he is abruptly dropped or cut off, with the result of experiences being incomplete. To help prepare for the ending, the adult should let him know shortly before the last five minutes how much time is left. This will give him some time to complete his communication and think about the ending. During the last five minutes, the room should be restored to its original condition. This helps to give a sense of containment and that the meeting has not been overwhelmed. For many reasons the child may find the tidying away difficult. If the child is asked to tidy away whatever he has been doing, this could feel like having to be responsible for his own communication. If the communication has been difficult, it could also feel like being forced to make reparation for it. This could then block communication in further meetings. The adult needs to take the responsibility for receiving and containing the child's communication by tidying up at the end. This also leaves room for the child to make reparation by joining in, if he is ready to do that. If he does not want to join in, he may be able to watch the adult doing this or decide to leave the room. The other adults in the house should be ready to receive the child when he leaves the meeting.

Supervision and communication outside of the meeting

It may be very difficult at times for the adult to work with the child's communication. This can lead to the adult protecting herself by defending against the communication. To help the process, it is essential that the adult has a supervisor who is able to help her think about the meeting and the child's communication. Having this support can be of great help when things are difficult and the adult may feel a stronger container by knowing someone is available for her. The supervisor and adult might also benefit for similar reasons by having access to a consultant child psychotherapist or other appropriately trained and qualified person.

Another aspect of work outside of the meeting is the relationship between the adult meeting the child and the other adults working with the child. Both will need to work together to create a sense of holding for the child. If the adult meeting the child has knowledge of how he is, including information about significant events, this can help focus the adult's attention and help make sense of his communication. The information needs to be known about but kept at the back of the mind as it could also cloud the adult's perception or receptivity. To create a sense of effective containment the adult who met the child will talk about the meetings with the other adults working with the child. There could be positive developments or worrying concerns that are helpful for them to know about. This communication will give the child a sense of things being connected for him. He will be able to use different situations how he wants to, but the adults involved are able to hold the whole of him together by talking and thinking about him with each other. The child may ask whether adults do talk about his meetings. It is positive to let him know that they do so it helps them to think about him. However, we should ensure that adults do not use information about the meetings directly with him or treat him in any way that could inhibit his use of the meetings.

The size and situation of the meeting room

The room needs to be big enough to play in and for there to be the feeling of space between the child and adult, but not so big that the room evokes feelings of being lost. The room should be situated in a location that feels safe without being easily impinged upon. The room should not be able to be easily seen into from the outside. For the meeting room to be used most effectively it should not be used for other purposes. If the room has other associations for the child and adult, this could be distracting. For example, an association such as being taken to the room to sort out difficulties might be unhelpful for the child.

The basic decor of the room should feel warm and well cared for. Colors that evoke strong feelings should not be used. Obviously, to some extent, this is a matter of taste, though pastel colors are probably the safest.

Contents of the room

First, we shall establish a framework to work within and then look at some useful materials and furnishing for meeting rooms. The effective use of these two aspects will help to facilitate the meeting.

It is most important in meetings that the child decides how materials should be used and what they represent. Too much descriptive detail can predetermine their character and not lend them to imaginative use. The materials should be readily available and easy to make use of, not jumbled up or be so many as to be overwhelming. How the adult feels about the materials in the room also needs attention. The adult needs to preside over the setting and work with whom she is comfortable. The meeting room should only have materials in it that the adult feels confident about managing safely or without creating an unmanageable mess. If the adult is anxious about either of these reasons then her receptivity will be affected. In addition, the child could feel unsafe and this may block his communication. As a number of adults use the same room, there needs to be consistency as to what is in the room. The adults need to discuss and agree about this, reaching a decision that they are happy about.

Furnishing

This should be simple and comfortable.

Chairs: Comfortable chairs with arms give a sense of holding. Two is probably the best number; more can give the impression of someone missing or of emptiness.

Carpet: This should be comfortable to play on.

Soft cushions: These give a feeling of softness, good for playing on the floor and for using in play, jumping on, hitting.

Table: This is for playing and drawing on. Also, it helps fill the space between the child and adult. This may feel safer than an empty space.

Pictures: They are not necessary if the room feels warm and pleasant to be in. If they are used, they should be simple and not too distracting.

Clock: The clock can symbolically represent the meeting time with a beginning, middle and end. It also allows the child to see the time and does not force him to be dependant on the adult. It reduces the potential for the child to feel controlled by the adult.

Materials

We shall now look at some materials that are useful for helping communication and give indicators of their potential symbolic use. Their use is, however, as unlimited as the imagination of the child using them.

Domestic and wild animals: These can be used to represent instinctual life. An assortment of 10 or 20 should be enough to represent big, small, fierce, wild and cuddly. If they are mixed together then the child can decide for himself what each one is. For instance, he could have a domestic lion and a wild hamster!

Fences: These can be used in play to represent containing, separating, dividing or trapping. Fences should be simple and easy to put together.

Bricks: These can be used in play for building, making walls or bridges. They have the disadvantage of being potentially dangerous.

Cars: These can be used in play to represent instinctual life – destruction, crashing, out of control, carrying, being stuck (in a traffic jam), speed or getting lost.

Human figures: There needs to be a range of sizes, male and female, black and white, enough to represent the child's family life and others. These figures can be used to tell stories as well as to represent instinctual life.

Sand: This has extensive potential for symbolic play. Careful thought needs giving to whether sand feels manageable or not, should it be wet or dry. Wet and dry sand trays can be used. If water is used then that should be in the room at the start of the meeting.

String: This can be used in play to represent joining, unraveling, tying knots and connecting. It is also easily used with other objects for different purposes.

Telephones: These can be used to communicate with the adult, to tell a story or to play at being different people.

Mirror: Reflections can be used in symbolic play, making things disappear and appear, reflecting what is there. Looking at a reflection of himself can be part of a child's developing sense of self.

Tea set: This can be used to represent the experiences of food and feeding, organizing, containing or filling. Stories can be told around mealtimes and tea parties.

Assortment of personal materials: These could be things like pens, crayons, pencils, paper, glue, Sellotape, rubber, plasticine. All of these readily lend themselves to different kinds of communication.

If each child has his own box of these materials, he then has personal ownership rather than everything being communal. He has the opportunity to make his own things, which can be taken away with him or looked after by the adult and brought back to the next meeting. This can give the child a sense of control, which feels safer for him. It may enable the experience of the meeting to be held onto and have a transitional quality linking one meeting to the next. The child's own box of materials should be looked after by the adult specifically for the meeting and should always be brought to the meeting.

The recording of children's individual meetings

The issue of recording therapeutic communication with children is complex because the nature of the work falls between internal and external reality, fantasy and objective reality. In general, the statutory requirement of recording in residential child care is concrete and factual.

Meetings with children are to facilitate communication from the child about his inner world reality and to allow him to play, which again will touch on that reality. The relationship between inner and outer reality in this communication will be variable. The adult meeting with the child has the task of being receptive to his communication in whatever form it takes and attempting to make sense of it. The adult also maintains certain boundaries around his communication, such that he will not physically hurt himself or the adult.

If at any time during a meeting a child discloses anything of a serious nature, about himself, other children, adults or his family, the adult will need to be clear about what the child is saying and act upon it accordingly, while ensuring an accurate recording of the communication is made. This can also include telling the child that other adults will need to know what he has said. More generally, the adult will communicate with other adults about the child's communication as part of the teamwork around his treatment. This is done thoughtfully so that the child does not experience any intrusion.

As children's meetings are not mainly about the communication of concrete external reality, it is not appropriate to record them in the logbook or on daily diary sheets. These are a legal document recording factual events in each child's life. To record a child's communication and play during his meetings in these documents is potentially confusing. As other people as well as the child have access to this information, there are also matters connected to privacy and confidentiality. As long as there are clear boundaries, the meetings provide children with a protected space within which they can freely communicate and play. Whoever is writing in the logbook or diary sheet can give a summary of a child's day, which includes his meeting, without going into the detail of exactly what he said or did in it.

The use of dolls and other figures in children's meetings

Dolls and other figures are often used in therapeutic work with children. The types of dolls vary significantly in their descriptive and suggestive quality. Some of the children had been asking for comic book-style 'hero' figures to play with in their meetings.

We questioned how much it matters if the dolls or play figures are more expressive rather than neutral, and whether the use of 'hero' type figures could open up more communication. More neutral type figures do not prescribe the expression of particular feelings or action. The feeling of wanting more 'exciting' things in the meeting room could be connected to the difficulty of the work involved in meeting a particular child. The most important thing in the meeting is the grown-up's receptivity to the child's communication. Sometimes meetings are hard work and it is difficult to stick with feelings of boredom, uncertainty of what is going on or that nothing may be happening. Important work can be happening while the child is doing seemingly very repetitive or boring things. This needs to be balanced by the possibility that the meeting is stuck and the repetition is avoidance. Careful thought about this is necessary.

Talking groups

Talking groups were a key part of the therapeutic approach and would happen in each house in small groups of three to four children. The talking group approach is particularly helpful for traumatized children who find it difficult to communicate in a group, and is for small groups of three to four children.

The history of talking groups

They were first used during Dockar-Drysdale's time at the Mulberry Bush School, of which she was head, and then the Cotswold Community. Some of the central ideas behind them were explained by her:

> There was, at this time, a disquieting split in the staff group – not openly discussed, but deeply felt. The children responded to this unspoken split by setting up a secret delinquent subculture... We the grown-ups talked about this difficult situation and agreed that the best hope seemed to be in the opening up of communication in the school. Accordingly, we set up what we now always call 'talking groups' of children, each group talking with a member of staff. The aim was to re-establish talking between children and between children and grown-ups. (Dockar-Drysdale 1990e, p.33)

In the same publication Dockar-Drysdale (1990d) also describes how in some groups the children's teddies or puppets (which she states were transitional objects) were used to communicate as a way in which the children 'as themselves' would not have been able to do. This happened organically and came from the group of children.

> Morning meetings of total groups (staff and children) had not proved successful... It now seemed that, while integrated boys could communicate in this sort of setting, unintegrated boys were unable to tolerate the high

> degree of stress, becoming disruptive, withdrawn or panicky... For the purpose of inter-communication, I suggested the introduction of very small groups (four boys to one adult). (p.153)
>
> Within the talking groups, matters to do with inner reality can surface safely. These groups have no part to play in management, that is no decisions are reached – the aim is not to make decisions but to facilitate open communication. (p.158)

Dockar-Drysdale emphasizes how important the reliability of these groups is, in terms of who is in the group, when and where they happen and their duration. She also says:

> Every boy should have opportunities for individual and group communication daily. This is the only answer to unintegrated subculture and acting out. (p.158)
>
> Unintegrated boys need a structure to contain: (1) regular small talking groups (2) individual communication with a grown-up and (3) immediate communication in context. (p.158)

What is the nature of communication in these groups?

Listening to each other is central. The experience of being listened to and thought about is a key aspect of the provision. We also wondered about the experience for children of actually being in a small group that is contained. The group might go through difficulties together, but may also achieve enjoyable experiences of being together – for instance, a shared story, perhaps both poignant and humorous, gathering everyone's attention. Each person in the group may get a sense of contributing something positive to the group at these times.

Some groups may communicate more through games rather than just talking and listening. If the group uses games, they should include the whole group together, allow for spontaneity and encourage attentiveness to each other's contribution. There must be the opportunity for each person to communicate something about himself.

The potential use of house group meetings

Group meetings are central to the therapeutic community (Rose 1990). Daily group meetings were established in all of the houses. House meetings or children's meetings are now also a central aspect of residential child care in general and are seen by the National Care Standards Commission as key to ensuring that children are fully involved in the running of the home.

The functions of group meetings are:

- to focus on 'what is going on' for individuals and the group as a whole;
- for anyone to raise an issue for discussion and thinking about;
- for passing on information and working on it;
- to make collective decisions;
- for planning the day.

The underlying value of these functions

An essential part of our work is to encourage open communication. The group meeting can symbolically represent this process. To do this the meeting must create the opportunity and encourage each individual (children and grown-ups) to speak openly. By the end of the meeting, each person should have been asked individually at some point if they have anything to say. This shows that each person's contribution is wanted and valued. If an individual does not want to speak, he will have been given the opportunity and had his wish respected. Giving an opportunity for each individual to express his own opinion or experience in a group meeting helps develop a sense of personal boundaries and identity. Statements such as 'there seems to be such and such a feeling in the group, how do others feel?' promote a sense of curiosity and reflection, rather than the certainty coming from more definite and fixed statements. At the same time, there could be occasions when someone remains silent in a challenging way, perhaps to maintain a position of power.

For some children, being in a group will be very difficult. It is necessary to remember that about some individuals and provide them with a sense of individual attention. Thinking about who should sit next to each child and which individual children grown-ups are focusing on in each meeting can help to do this.

Group meetings can also provide a focus for working on matters like scapegoating, splitting, pairing and bullying. Different bits of reality or experience can be brought together and tested in the group meeting. Through this process, it is more likely that issues which can be hidden or lost in the day-to-day situation will be brought into the open.

How do adults work together in group meetings?

While there is increasing clarity on the potential value of group meetings, achieving this potential is a complex and challenging task. If the difficulties are not acknowledged, understood and worked with consistently by the adults, the meetings are not likely to succeed in their task and become established within the house culture.

Each house has regular daily group meetings with children. The content of the meetings is normally focused on sharing information, making plans and working on matters related to the daily life of the group and the individuals in it. The adult who is managing the house for the day tends to chair each group meeting. There is an expectation in the staff team that all adults will contribute to the work in these meetings and not just leave this responsibility with the manager. However, a dynamic often develops where the manager takes on the role of single-handedly challenging all the children present for their actions and behavior. It might not be clear what the therapeutic aim of this is and it can feel quite punitive. Sometimes the meeting evokes peer pressure towards a particular child. A child can feel that this is punitive and frightening. It is more appropriate when the peer pressure comes spontaneously from the child group. It is essential that room is left for a child to make reparation and that he is not completely pushed into a corner. There needs to be room for each child to contribute to the group in a positive way.

If the group and the manager become confrontational, it can be difficult for other adults to contribute. Taking a similar viewpoint as the manager can feel like reinforcing an already powerful situation, which can lead to a polarization of 'us and them' feelings between children and adults. To give a different viewpoint to the manager can appear to undermine her, especially if she has taken a confrontational or harsh position. Bold statements can be difficult to step down from. This ambivalence can result in adults maintaining an uncomfortable silence. Everyone in these situations, children and adults, could feel isolated and unsupported by each other. The way in which the adults work together with the children in the group may also reflect the way they communicate with each other as a team. For instance, if the team cannot listen to each other and consider different points of view in team meetings, they are likely to feel even more vulnerable and defensive in meetings with children.

The dynamics and feelings among the children can also get into the staff team. If this is not consciously recognized, different adults might begin to act out different roles in relation to each other. In particular, the manager chairing the group meeting can be the focus for powerful projections from children and adults. During times when the group is having difficulties, harsh punitive feelings may be projected onto the manager. There could be unrealistic expectations on her to 'sort things out'. At the same time, if these feelings are projected then there will also be a fear of the manager becoming harsh or aggressive, as she is carrying the feelings that have been disowned by others in the group. If the manager takes on this role, the children may feel under attack and could be perceived by other adults as being in the need of protection. If an adult responds in a protective way, then children and adults could perceive her to be siding with the children. Scenarios such as this are regularly part of the group process, and depending on how they are worked with they have the potential to either reinforce or modify defensive and repetitive behavior patterns. Given the nature of our task, we can expect these difficulties to be typical. The therapeutic task is how we try to understand and work with them.

As described earlier it is important that everyone can contribute to the meeting. If there is a difference of opinion, this can be expressed and discussed. To offer a different opinion is not the same as dismissing someone else's. For instance, each person may have a different experience of what it feels like to be in the group at any one point in time. This is a healthier reality than one person telling the whole group how it is in the group, without being open to different points of view. Ideally, the group meeting should evoke a sense of curiosity towards each other's experiences. This can help a child to develop a sense of personal boundaries, by having his own experience acknowledged but by also recognizing other people's experience. Groups that are fraught with high levels of anxiety tend to move towards a closed group with polarized points of view such as one is either right or wrong, in or out. In these groups, there can be a great pressure to comply with one point of view and there is the tendency for people to speak on behalf of others.

While meetings should be as open as possible in these areas, adults do need to be clear and consistent about policies that have been adopted by the team. It is not helpful to disagree with each other about these things in meetings with children. Where an adult is expressing a different opinion or perception about something, we should also consider the motivation for doing this. What is the difference about? Is it best to raise it in the meeting or outside of it? How can the opinion be put across most helpfully? Given that group work is such a central part of the task and that it is complex and difficult, it is useful for the adult team to find time for discussing their experiences with each other. Although everyone in the team is rarely together in a meeting with children, a meeting could be discussed in detail by the whole team, exploring and attempting to understand interactions, roles and positions taken in the meeting.

Time boundaries and working through difficulties

In any meeting, the issue of time boundaries is significant to the task of the meeting. In a residential setting where meetings happen regularly and have to be integrated into the daily routine, it is important to achieve a balance between a clear boundary and some flexibility.

Each house has regular group meetings for purposes we have described previously. Some houses have had meetings lasting for well over an hour. Generally, meetings last for roughly half an hour after tea. Should group meetings have a predetermined appropriate duration? The length of these meetings is not explicit but adults should be conscious of how long they should be. Sometimes, if there is not much work to be done and the planning part of the meeting goes smoothly, the meeting may not take so long. On the other hand, if it seems necessary to work with the group before other activities can take place and this work is difficult with a lot of disruption, the meeting could take longer.

From a therapeutic point of view, the adults may feel that certain matters need acknowledging and working on in the group. They might also feel the need to work on the sense of containment in the group until it feels safe to get on with other things. On some occasions, the meeting breaks down and the group or part of the group has to be managed within the room, until they are more settled. When the feeling in the group is particularly problematic, meetings can be used to try to shift the feel of the group and create a better atmosphere. However, this needs careful thought as the group atmosphere can also deteriorate during a prolonged meeting. It could be argued that if it seems everything is going smoothly the meeting should be longer to get more in touch with matters lying under the surface. If the group is difficult, a focus on activity that supports the children's ability to function may help to manage anxiety. The group's capacity to work on difficulties will also be greater when the group is functioning positively.

We can expect a group of emotionally unintegrated children to be self-punishing. These feelings could be projected by children in a group meeting and the adults become drawn into collusion, by reacting in a harsh and punitive way. In such a situation, it is likely the children will respond by attacking the adults. An entrenched 'us and them' situation can soon develop. We should think carefully about these dynamics and the roles we feel ourselves taking on.

A team can feel that it is very important to be able emotionally to hold a whole group in a meeting. If this is not possible or does not work, the adults might feel quite persecuted as if they are failing. This can develop into a determination to make the group sit together. The need to feel in charge in this way could be an anxiety of the adults, as well as one they are picking up from the children and sometimes from other sources, such as staff outside of the home, parents and social workers. This could also be linked to an anxiety that the only way to ensure the group is safe is, literally, to make sure no one has the chance to be out of sight. Though this might be connected to concern for the children, it may not actually help to manage anxiety or improve the feeling of safety. It might not always be realistic or necessary to have whole group meetings every day. Assessment of what work can be done safely in the group should take place. Even if a team agrees that it is necessary to preserve the sense of the group together as a whole, the length of time could be shortened. In these situations the adults could explain to the children that 'we have been thinking about this together, we may have got into a bad habit about meetings and think it could be more helpful to meet in this way.'

One of our underlying principles is that children should not be punished. The Children Act 1989 (DH 1991) also supports this idea in relation to prohibited measures such as withholding of basic needs. In the same way, children should not be stopped from playing purely as a reaction to something they have done. When we stop a child or group from moving into this type of activity, we should be clear about our reasons. It can be difficult to move from the position of disapproval towards a child to one of providing an opportunity for play. There are different possibilities – we should acknowledge when something has happened that is not okay and express some straightforward feeling about it. Depending on the situation and individual child, varying degrees of work may be appropriate to try to help a child think about what he has done. Again, we do need to be wary of taking on the role of abusive carer with unrealistic expectations. To what extent is it the child's responsibility to change and what the adult's? Similarly, we could take on the role of a neglectful carer, who deprives or hurts a child by not paying attention, failing to create safety by letting too much go. These dynamics could be a reenactment of children's previous experiences.

It is positive that a range of feelings can be acknowledged in relation to situations or behavior that we find difficult. For example, there is a tendency to get in the habit of thinking anger is the only appropriate feeling in response to dangerous behavior.

When things are difficult, how do we ensure that this does not swamp everything else that is going on? Even at the most difficult times there may be some positive things happening that should be acknowledged. Partly this is connected to the idea of not reinforcing the notion that the only way of getting attention is by being difficult. Care is needed to avoid feeding into a child's low self-esteem and sense that he is bad and worthless. Explaining what he has done and the consequence of it can potentially boost him in that it encourages him to think about the reality of his actions.

We need to have a realistic expectation of how long a group can be expected to meet. This will vary according to the developmental stage of the group and other variable factors. It can also be appropriate to have different expectations for different children. Adults should think carefully about what is happening in a meeting and the reasons for their approach. This work should also be monitored and discussed as part of the team's work together.

Working with children who find it extremely difficult to be in groups

The children at the Community lived in groups of up to ten children and this was used to a full extent in the therapeutic approach. However, there would be situations where being in a group seemed extremely difficult for a particular child. This would tend to happen most when a child was new. As group living was central to the therapeutic approach, responding to the needs of these children was challenging.

The phrase 'pre-group' has been used to describe children who find it extremely difficult to be in a group. Emotionally unintegrated children have not developed a sense of self that enables them to relate to other people as individuals. They require a huge amount of support in their relationships with others. Relating to others can only be sustained with the ego support provided by an adult. Clearly, the more unintegrated the child the greater the support needed. Some of the children we work with require one-to-one attention to function in a group. In these cases the grown-up is providing the ego rather than supporting the child's ego, as it is not possible to support what is not there (Dockar-Drysdale 1990d, p.157). Whether the child is able to be in the group or not will be determined by his own emotional capacity, the nature of the group and the support provided by boundaries, structure and adult preoccupation.

Different group settings could be more or less demanding for a child. For example, being in a group in the school is different from being in a group in the house. The level of support he needs may vary between the two. We should aim to provide a plan for each child that enables him to be in his different groups. A lot of thought needs to be paid to individual need, but also to the nature of the group. For example, at a time when a house was finding it impossible to hold group meetings due to the level of disruption, it decided to split the group into two smaller groups. This still provided the experience of being in a group and was realistically manageable. Over time, this experience could be internalized so the group gradually became able to come back together.

It is difficult for some children to be in a class as this also involves managing the separation from the house and carers. It is necessary that we make a realistic assessment of what the more unintegrated children can manage and how much support is needed. In some cases, a high degree of individual attention is needed in school and this could include individual time outside of the class group. To maintain the educational focus the individual time could also be linked into the National Curriculum.

Chapter 7

Language

The language we use with children and the way we talk with children is a key aspect of our work. A consistent approach based upon the needs of the children can have a powerful effect in meeting those needs. If we are not consistent and do not think about the effect of what we say and how we say it, this can be confusing to the child. This is especially difficult in settings where a large team is working with the children. At times, we find that our language begins to echo some of the past experiences of the child. For example, we may find ourselves reacting in a harsh or punitive manner.

The use of language

Using helpful words in work with children is a challenging task that needs careful thought. We need to consider being consistent, using words the child can understand, not using institutionalized jargon, and keeping our language clear when under stress.

Sometimes we might say something to a child that implies that his behavior is a fixed part of himself, such as telling a child he is violent, rather than his behavior is violent. The children we work with often have negative views of themselves and can be anxious that they are bad and destructive. We need to be careful not to confirm a child's worst fears about himself. It is possible at the same time to let him know what we think about his behavior. If we were to tell a child that his behavior is violent, that also implies there is a choice he is making or can be helped to make about his behaviour, whereas if we say he is violent, the implication is that it feels more permanent and potentially overwhelming. The word 'violent' is a powerful one though using it might help a child distinguish between aggression and violence.

Aggression can be used to refer to self-assertive behavior, sometimes appropriately and sometimes inappropriately expressed. Violence usually refers to an act that is designed to hurt or cause damage and tends mostly to be a negative act. We should think carefully how a child might perceive the use of different words and to what extent he can distinguish meaning and make sense of powerful language without becoming confused and overwhelmed.

Words such as 'abuser', 'predator', 'bully' or 'liar' have harsh undertones and tend also to label those to whom they refer. They also imply a degree of organization and conscious intent that normally would be associated with emotional integration. These types of words blur the difference between an unintegrated child's behavior and the behavior of abusive adults. For example, there could be children whom we are unable to work with in a way that feels safe, but that does not make a particular child an abuser. Similarly, we would not tend to refer to an infant as being abusive, though the parent or carer might actually feel as if she is on the receiving end of abuse. It is important to recognize these feelings and think about them. As well as helping a child think about his behavior and take responsibility for it, there is also a need for the carer to make sense of the child and his behavior. This needs to be done in a way that the child can understand and potentially make use of. There will be differences in how we do this work with different children depending on their stages of emotional development.

A useful way to describe and think about the expression of feelings in general can be to say a person is showing a particular feeling or behavior, rather than that he is being something or other. For example, we could say a child is showing us anger. This way of thinking also implies that he may have other feelings but anger is the one he is showing us now. It might also lead us on to think about the feelings that other children and adults are showing or not showing and to consider the role of a child in the group. Do certain children tend to show a particular feeling on behalf of the group?

At times, we use words that are a sort of shorthand. For example, 'Daniel was kicking off' or 'Adam has trashed his room.' These types of phrases assume a shared understanding of their meaning and are actually quite often used to mean different things. Also they do not draw attention to the detail of what a child was doing and why. For instance, a child smearing toothpaste all over his room and a child breaking everything provided by his carer may have quite different meanings. Words like 'trash' and 'kicking off' have an element of excitement to them that can distract from thinking about the meaning of the behavior. We also use unhelpful jargon at times when talking with children, for example, words such as 'boundary'.

As well as thinking about the way we talk with children, we should also think about the way we communicate with each other. It is most helpful that we try to use language that describes as clearly as possible what is actually happening. Rather than say that a child is being violent, say what he is actually doing. A log entry that says a child was violent does not tell us a great deal compared with the facts of what he actually did. If we try to use clear language that is understandable to everyone, it will also help us to think more clearly about our work. This is not always easy, as we may not necessarily understand what is happening and might feel confused or overwhelmed. At these times, it may feel safer to use jargon or shorthand-type of words as they tend to feel familiar and, to some extent, they depersonalize experience by ordering things into a sort of pattern.

Things we say to children that feel inappropriate

When we are experiencing the emotional impact of work with traumatized children, it is difficult to talk with them without slipping into 'defensive' language, for example, language that is reactive to the child and self-protective rather than a more open and thoughtful response. This language can quickly develop and become an institutionalized way of talking with children.

The inappropriate things that we say fall into a number of categories:

- the use of confusing, nonsensical jargon, for example, telling a young child, 'you are splitting and need to stop it';
- telling a child in quite an imposing way how he is, for example, 'You are a sad, sad child' or 'You are in a mess' or 'You are not listening to me.' These comments are also often said in an accusatory tone;
- telling a child that he needs to sort or work things out, which is also often said with an underlying threat or sense of revenge;
- telling a child who had been in a panic that he was in control of himself and ought to think more about what he was doing.

We acknowledge that we are more likely to say or use inappropriate language when we are having difficulties in thinking, when we are at the end of our tether. However, we need to have clear and consistent expectations of how we talk with children. This makes it harder to slip into bad habits. We should always try to use language that will be understandable to the child. Language should not be too imprisoning, so the child has no room to respond or question what is being said. A child may hear things quite concretely and misunderstand complex language.

When we tell a child we want to talk to him because of his difficult behavior, we need to be careful that we are actually expressing concern, trying to understand what is going on and to help him with it, rather than trying to punish him. How much should we expect children, especially the more emotionally unintegrated ones, to think or talk about themselves? There is a risk of encouraging a response from the child, where he will just do or say what he thinks is necessary to keep the grown-up happy.

If we make mistakes in the things we say to children, we should acknowledge this. Saying sorry to the child can be complicated, if it leaves him feeling the grown-up is expecting something from him in return, for instance, if the child feels the grown-up wants to be forgiven or for the child to like him. It may be more straightforward just to acknowledge the mistake rather than to apologize.

The use of humor

It is often said by staff involved in caring professions that it is important to have a sense of humor. However, it is not so usual to question what we mean when we use the word 'humor'. Humor is positive if it is genuinely enjoyable to all involved. It is beneficial for children to be able to make us laugh and to experiment in this way, discovering what we find funny. However, the use of humor and jokes also need thinking about carefully.

Jokes are sometimes used to exclude others and this is no less so with a child who may feel excluded by grown-ups joking together. A child may not have the capacity to respond to or understand a grown-up's joke, which might leave him feeling belittled. If the joking involves grown-ups winding each other up, it would then be difficult to stop children from doing this with each other. It could also be confusing for a child if he had been told to stop doing this. If a joke is made of a child (or grown-up), he may feel upset by this and stupid (as a joke is meant to be funny rather than upsetting). Jokes are sometimes used in this way as a disguised form of aggression. Sarcasm in particular is used in this way and gives a double message that can be confusing. Teasing is often hurtful and aggressive, and difficult for children who are not easily able to distinguish between fantasy play and external reality. If the teasing is suggesting something to be different than it actually is, this might feel like a lie to the child. For example, teasing often involves pretending or playing a trick, which may be difficult for some children to understand.

We should not call a child anything that he is not, for instance, nicknaming or ridiculing a personal characteristic. Nicknaming may be appropriate if it follows the child having a clear sense of his real name and the nickname is an affectionate term which he likes. If the child calls himself something or pretends to be something that he is not, we should not then take that up ourselves. This is to help the child establish his sense of identity. Children with low self-esteem may also put themselves down and we should be careful not to go along with this. The children we work with have a fragile sense of self, if any at all, and have had overwhelming experiences, leading to states of confusion. It is essential that in our language and actions we are clear in saying and doing what we mean. Language should be simple and clear without hidden messages.

The use of shouting

Shouting has a tendency to become a habit from time to time in work with traumatized children. What are we trying to communicate to children when we shout? Is it a wish to be heard above the chaos? Shouting can feel bullying, frightening and intimidating. When is shouting appropriate and useful? Can it be an appropriate way to bring about order?

By not shouting, we might enable others to listen more. Rather than raising voices, talking more quietly can be effective. It is hard to listen to bellowing. There can be different perceptions of children and grown-ups shouting. A grown-up's shouting may be perceived as an expression of authority and anger, but with children it is more often seen as feelings being acted out. There are different types of shouting. For example, authoritative, out of control, release of aggression and frightened. Sometimes a culture develops where authority is based on shouting. Often this feels like a male type of authority which then becomes a model for all staff and children.

Shouting can be a way of trying to get through to someone. If a child is trying to get through to us emotionally and we are unreceptive, his frustration could lead him to try increasingly extreme ways of trying to get through. If we remain unreceptive, we may feel increasingly irritated with his attempts to get under our skin. We might then end up reacting by shouting back at him in an intrusive way. If there is a lot of shouting, the atmosphere can feel tense and on edge. This is not conducive to the calm, receptive environment associated with primary provision. This is especially noticeable at times such as bedtime and waking-up time.

Whether shouting is useful or not largely depends upon the motive. Shouting to establish a power base, the verbal equivalent of hitting, is not constructive. Shouting can be a way of conveying real emotive feelings such as anger or worry. In this case, we need to be careful that this is also how the child perceives it. Shouting can be used as a way of bringing someone to his or her senses, or to warn of danger. However, this is difficult to judge as it could also have the opposite effect. Ideally, we try to work with children by developing relationships, so children feel emotionally held. In this situation, a child may choose not to do something rather than be scared to do it.

To ensure that we do not develop a habit of shouting or other ways of responding ineffectively, it is necessary that we continually think about this complex area. It is also important to examine the interrelationship between our work with children, staff and our personal life. A disproportionate amount of shouting or confrontation in one area might be a displacement of matters that need working on elsewhere.

Chapter 8

Delinquent Excitement and Subculture

Winnicott (1956b) made the connection that antisocial behavior, sometimes described as 'delinquent' behavior, could be seen as hopeful. Antisocial behavior is prevalent in traumatized children and our understanding and response to this is crucial in meeting the child's needs. As Winnicott wrote:

> The antisocial tendency implies hope. Lack of hope is the basic feature of the deprived child who, of course, is not all the time being antisocial. In the period of hope, the child manifests an antisocial tendency. (p.309)

> The understanding that the antisocial tendency is an expression of hope is vital in the treatment of children who show the antisocial tendency. Over and over again one sees the moment wasted, or withered, because of mismanagement or intolerance. This is another way of saying that the treatment of the antisocial tendency is not psychoanalysis but management, a going to meet and match the moment of hope. (p.309)

> When there is an antisocial tendency there has been a true deprivation (not a simple privation); that is to say there has been a loss of something good that has been positive in the child's experience up to a certain date, and that has been withdrawn; the withdrawal has extended over a period of time longer than that over which the child can keep the memory of the experience alive. (p.309)

Delinquency as a sign of hope

We had read Winnicott's (1956b) paper 'The antisocial tendency' prior to this discussion. This is a seminal paper in helping us to understand antisocial behavior and therapeutic work with emotionally deprived children.

At times when children are acting in an antisocial and destructive manner, there can be a strong feeling within adults that this behavior is a sign they are doing a bad job and things are going wrong. There might be a wish to eliminate the behavior or acting out. Winnicott's paper looks at the hopeful aspect of delinquency or antisocial behavior. If we take a less reactive response to the behavior, we may be able to see the communication and need behind the behavior. Due to the disturbing nature of antisocial behavior, it can be difficult to hold onto this position and we can easily become overwhelmed and hopeless. There is often a need to manage antisocial behavior. This can be done in a way that also tries to understand such behavior, though the balance is difficult to keep. It can seem as if management and therapy or intervention and understanding are becoming polarized, rather than part of the same thing.

A child or young person whose behavior is antisocial may be trying to evoke a response from the environment around him, as part of what he is looking for could be the need for boundaries and appropriate management. The behavior could be seen as a signal or cry for help. If the behavior is destructive and anxiety-provoking, it might not be immediately possible or appropriate to focus on the meaning of the behavior. A key turning point often follows antisocial behavior, when those working with the child are able to think collectively about the behavior and what may be behind it. Antisocial behavior can be seen as the expression of a desire for something. For example, a child who steals may desire something good that he feels is missing and which he wishes to find. This could be the attention and love of a parental figure. It is not the stolen object itself that is desired but what it represents. If this need is recognized by a carer or parent, then rather than focus on the stealing in a reactive or punitive way, the carer who recognizes the child's need may be able to provide him with something, for example, food that the child can be excited about enjoying. It is not the food or thing in itself that is significant but what it represents between the child and carer.

If the need behind the antisocial behavior is misunderstood then the child may be responded to in a way that perpetuates the behavior. For example, if a child steals something and all the attention is on the stealing, he will not feel understood and may become increasingly antisocial in an attempt to evoke the desired response. If the opportunity to provide the desired response is repeatedly missed, the child could become quite hardened and focused on secondary gains associated with the antisocial behavior, for example, money or power.

The children we work with will also attack our attempts to think about and understand them. This is linked to their overwhelming sense of mistrust. While adults who are feeling retaliatory and punitive may show this in their response, children are also likely to attack the benign response. Children may react in a paranoid way to benign interpretations that adults make, as if they are being persecuted. Feelings such as persecution, hopelessness and despair may be projected or displaced onto the adults. There could be a tendency for the adults to take flight from these feelings rather than recognize them and continue working with them. Children may be testing to see whether adults can survive and continue to meet needs when they are faced with difficult and challenging behavior. When there are difficulties within the group, it is more likely that a split develops between children and adults with an 'us and them' type of feeling.

If there is little antisocial behavior in a group, this in itself does not mean therapeutic work is happening. For example, the group might be responding in a compliant way to a rigid style of management. There could be an overencouragement of children, giving a false but positive impression of how they feel (Winnicott 1960a).

The feelings involved in work with children and young people who are behaving delinquently can be powerful. When this becomes overwhelming, we may believe we can get rid of the behavior by getting rid of the child or young person. It seems that it becomes harder to think about the behavior when it is group rather than individual behavior. We have often been able to work with extreme behavior from individual children. When this type of behavior becomes more of a group phenomenon, there is a high level of anxiety and a fear for the safety of children. At these times, there is more of a limit in terms of how long the behavior can be lived and worked with before something is done to ensure that it stops. Often we try to isolate the 'storm center' who may be influencing the whole group, to work with him individually and to try to break the group pattern. When antisocial behavior becomes a group phenomenon, the secondary gains involved, such as power, status and excitement within the group, can become established quickly and the pattern of behavior difficult to break through.

This is very much the problem in residential treatment where one delinquent boy can become a 'hero' and 'storm center' (Redl 1966). Other children are so afraid of this boy that they dare not reveal what has been happening, even if they have been badly hurt and frightened. Dockar-Drysdale (1990f) argues, 'So I would be quite sure that direct and open communication is essential in every residential place, so that at no time will children or their caring people be dominated by collusive anxiety.' (p.146)

Working with delinquent excitement and subculture in groups of children

This can be a difficult and powerful happening in any group including a family. In residential homes, the difficulty often seriously challenges the safety of the group and can make therapeutic work seem impossible.

Some of the themes that emerge when there is excitement in the group are, first, children get into a pattern of running around together out of the adults' reach. This running around feels exciting and children say things like 'it is better than staying in the house', 'the house is boring' and 'I want to leave the Community.' The running around sometimes involves sexual talk or involvement between children; a sense of having adults on the run; destructive behavior, such as damaging things, stealing and breaking into buildings; dangerous or self-destructive behavior, such as climbing roofs and making suicidal gestures; and aggression towards adults who try to interrupt or intervene.

Second, once such a pattern gets into the house culture, it is difficult to break. How might we understand this type of behavior and respond to it in a way that helps break the pattern?

Third, delinquent excitement and subculture often seem to involve anxiety and self-provision. Children seem anxious and uncontained but try to find the solution themselves or with each other, often rejecting adult care. During periods of change, this is more likely as there is an increase in anxiety partly related to things being less secure and reliable. Changes, such as staff leaving in particular, can create a sense of unreliability and mistrust. This will be especially so if leaving is sudden, unplanned or without sufficient time to work on them in advance. After a staff member leaves, the house will need to mourn the loss involved. These feelings can be difficult to acknowledge and hold onto. Delinquent excitement might be a way of taking flight and warding off these feelings.

Fourth, if the staff team has difficult or angry feelings towards the person who has left, the team may not be receptive to feelings of sadness and loss related to that person. Good memories might be difficult to acknowledge. If children sense that adults are not receptive to understanding these feelings, flight will be even more likely. The children may feel that the adults are rejecting them. They may feel excluded by this and let the adults know by making them feel excluded. If adults respond in a way that children feel to be punitive, this can reinforce these feelings. It sometimes feels like we quickly forget staff who have left, while new staff are quickly integrated into the team. This is highlighted by the great difficulty we have in actually making plans for future contact with someone who is leaving.

There are other matters that could be connected with delinquent excitement. If the excitement is centered on something specific like sexual involvement, this may be because the children feel the adults are unable to manage and understand this problem. So, becoming sexually involved with each other might be a way of showing it can be managed and making it less frightening.

Other matters may be connected to the need for appropriate limits and boundaries; the need for primary provision and emotional holding; breakdowns in communication; unacknowledged feelings in staff teams being acted out by children; unstimulating and uninteresting cultures; and collusive anxiety in the staff team. Collusive anxiety is where an adult may turn a 'blind eye' rather than confront the reality, due to a fear of possible reaction (Dockar-Drysdale 1990f).

In each case, it is necessary to consider what the background factors are and what form the excitement and subculture actually takes, including the feelings it evokes in staff. Working with this can be difficult because it often provokes anxiety. It can require a great deal of emotional energy and resources to work and stick with the difficulty in a way that is helpful, rather than react to it in a way that generates further anxiety and excitement.

Working with excitement in the group about drugs

In groups of young people excitement about drugs can often arise and can be difficult to make sense of. Many of the matters raised are also relevant to work with individual young people.

Members of the group may be using drugs. Adults need to be attentive to the warning signs, such as physical symptoms. The dangers should be explained to children in a way that is appropriate to their understanding.

Talk of drugs can feel exciting, secretive and exclusive. This might be a way of letting adults know that a young person or the group feel excluded or want to be more in the center of things. The secrecy and danger involved may mirror a sense by young people that what adults do, they do not know about, is forbidden, and so must be exciting and dangerous. Young people may think adults are having a good time and be envious of this. Drugs might be a way of creating their own good time. Teams need to work on these feelings. It may be helpful to acknowledge to the young people that it can be difficult for them not to know what adults are doing all the time, and to give children an opportunity to express feelings, concerns and fantasies about this.

Other matters that could also be connected are:

- The secrecy could be an attack on the culture of talking.
- Drugs might be a way of taking flight from difficulties.
- There may be a fear of losing control or emotionally disintegrating, which is being expressed through the talk of drugs.
- The excitement in the group could be connected to power and bullying.
- Drug excitement might be a form of self-provision, indicating needs are not being met.
- Addictive tendencies may be focused on drugs.
- Drugs may be a way of exploring and trying things out.
- If adults are overanxious or judgmental, it might be difficult for children to talk about or admit to any involvement or interest in drugs.

Finally, if young people ask adults questions such as 'have you taken drugs?' it can be helpful to explore the child's feelings, fantasies and concerns rather than talk about one's own experiences. The young person could want to find out what is 'normal' and what do adults do, so we should try not to respond too defensively even if, at times, the questions might feel quite intrusive.

While we have specifically discussed drugs, the same issues would apply to excitement about any illicit activity, like smoking, drinking alcohol, glue-sniffing, sex and pornography.

How do we work with aspects of youth culture that may be offensive?

Youth culture as part of the adolescent process of separation from parental figures and developing one's own identity inevitably contains aspects that can feel offensive. This can be seen as part of the separation and rejection process. In work with young people who have been traumatized by parents or carers, there is an additional complexity in trying to work out how to respond to this.

We had difficulties during a period when children were listening to music with offensive lyrics and had been behaving in an intimidating way.

Often these tapes have a warning that the material may be offensive. The music has lyrics with words such as 'nigger', 'slut' and 'bitch'. In particular, black people and women are denigrated. As well as listening to this music on their own, children swap tapes and play the music loudly in communal areas.

Music that is denigrating in this way should not be approved of. It is appropriate to say to children that we do not like to hear music like this in the house and we will not allow it. The reasons should be given but done in a way that allows for the possibility of exploring the children's interest in the music. This gives children a model of the way we think individuals and groups should be treated and respected.

There might be many reasons why children want to listen to and play different types of music:

- The music may belong to a youth culture with which a child wishes to identify as part of his individuation and separation from home. In general, identifying his own tastes will be part of his development as a person. In some cases, he might not fully appreciate the implications of the music.
- The music might be used in a rebellious way to express feelings towards authority and parental figures. This could also be part of separation, though it might feel aggressive and attacking or denigrating. In a group setting, this could feel like a subculture. The way feelings are expressed should be challenged or confronted. We might not necessarily disapprove of a child's feelings or thoughts but rather the way he expresses them.
- In discovering his own interests, a child may wish to share them with the adults he is close to and find out what they think. What do the adults like and dislike, approve of and understand?
- The offensive music the child listens to could be a way of him trying to manage or find a focus for powerful feelings. This could enable him to feel more in control of his feelings and less threatened by them.

If the music is not blatantly offensive, whether children listen to it, who with, where in the house and how loud it is can be discussed, taking into account different points of view. It is the same as the television programs we watch, comics and magazines children read, and computer games we play. On the one hand, in a treatment setting, we need to protect children from certain types of experience (protection from impingement, Dockar-Drysdale 1960b) but also leave enough space for exploring and discovering what the world is all about.

Tarot cards and other types of fortune-telling

Young people often become interested in fortune-telling and the occult through media such as Ouija boards and tarot cards. Where children have a fragile sense of the boundary between fantasy and reality this experience can be difficult to manage.

We had an instinctive feeling that fortune-telling was not a good idea or helpful to traumatized children. Fortune-telling can seem to be benign as with the daily horoscope but there are also associations with good and evil, witchcraft and the occult. Fortune-telling promotes a certain kind of thinking. It is valuable for us to talk about these things and help children explore matters they bring up. It is also of value for the staff team as a whole to be aware of these matters and talk about them together.

From a more theoretical point of view, the children we work with are in either a state of omnipotence, and unable to distinguish clearly between fantasy and reality (Winnicott 1960a, pp.145–146), or have only just reached emotional integration and are able to make this distinction. The unintegrated child has an illusion of being in control and his needs being met, as if by his magical wish. The newly integrated child is only just giving up this illusion and is facing the reality of not being in control in a magical way. To present him with the possibility of telling his fortune could make it difficult for him to hold onto this newly established reality and is potentially confusing. This could lead to a flight from reality, which might be difficult to manage. For instance, the attraction of magical solutions or escapes from reality may be more appealing than the responsibility of day-to-day life. Fortune-telling is not likely to be meaningful or helpful to the emotionally unintegrated child who is struggling to have an experience of being in the present.

Chapter 9

Authority, Consequences and Reparation

From the beginning, the Cotswold Community employed organizational consultants from the Tavistock Institute of Human Relations. The Community's management would use the consultancy to think about and try to make sense of their prevailing concerns and dynamics. On an occasion when the Community was struggling to attain authority in relation to some of the young people, we were considering the nature of authority with the Community's organizational consultant, Eric Miller. He suggested that authority was that which an infant would give to his mother after experiencing continuous responses by her to meet his need. This is a personal authority based in trust. We often find in our work with traumatized children that they are mistrustful of authority and attempts to impose authority have little effect. Authority that is based in a trusting relationship is also crucial in the development of concern and reparation. Where a child trusts the authority of an adult, it is possible to help the child begin to consider the consequences of his actions, in particular in relation to others. A child who is aware of consequences and who feels concern will begin to make reparation for destructive behavior. Reparation is central to therapeutic work with traumatized children.

Working with consequences

How do we work with the reality of the consequence of behavior and actions? This applies to both the work with children and between adults.

The reality of how our behavior and attitudes affect others is integral to the therapeutic approach with traumatized children. There can be a number of difficulties and matters to think about here.

In work with a child, we need to assess the extent to which he will be able to make use of being presented with external reality. This will be related to the stage he is at in his development and will influence not only what we present but how. However emotionally unintegrated a child is, it is not helpful that we deny reality, whether this is something concrete about his behavior or more subjective in terms of our feeling towards him. In a state of high anxiety or panic, a child will not have a real sense of what he is actually doing. For instance, he may defend himself by using denial or exaggerate the extent of his destructiveness through omnipotence. To help a child get a sense of external reality it is necessary to show him what he has actually done, when he is settled enough to see this and think about it. The phrase 'reality confrontation' is sometimes used to describe this area of work. It applies equally to pointing out to a child that he has not been destructive when he thinks he has, and to pointing out he has done something that he is denying. In this sense, reality confrontation is nonjudgmental and does not imply any particular tone to the confrontation.

The extent to which the reality is pushed strongly towards a child or suggested to him will depend upon his stage of development. Unintegrated children can be very limited in their capacity to perceive external reality. In these situations the adult will need to accept this and take responsibility for managing the situation. As a child becomes integrated we would expect him to have a greater sense of external reality and capacity to take responsibility for his own actions. This would include thinking about his behavior and feedback from others and making appropriate reparation.

We also need to make a judgment when the reality we are working with is that of how we feel about a child. For instance, if we feel very angry towards a child, how do we deal with this? If we are clear the anger is really to do with the child, the most straightforward thing to do would be to tell him, 'I am feeling angry with you because...' With unintegrated children the closer that this work can happen in relation to the particular situation, the more likely a child will be able to make a connection between the feeling and his behavior.

As a child becomes more integrated, he will be more able to understand that the impact of his behavior can be felt over time. For example, following a particularly difficult experience, often a child will ask an adult to do something, such as play a game, as if everything is okay. If everything is not okay, it would be unhelpful to the child for the adult to deny that to herself. The difficulty is in knowing what to say and how to explain this to the child.

With an integrated child, we should aim to stick with the difficulties until it feels that something has really been acknowledged and dealt with, even if that takes a few days. With a child who has difficulty holding onto feelings, there is a risk of him feeling that his behavior has been overwhelming and not recoverable from – that he cannot do anything about it and its effects are irretrievable. It might be possible in this situation to let the child know the difficulty has not just gone away, but it will not stop ordinary daily events from happening.

Where there are punitive feelings towards the child this can be difficult work. The idea of consequences can be used as a form of punishment. This is especially so if the consequence seems unconnected from the difficulty, for example, if a child was told he could not have his special time because he had run away. However, if he had run away just before his special time and it seemed urgent to sit and talk with him rather than have his special time straight away, this may be different.

As well as punitive responses, there can be difficulties in relation to collusive responses (Dockar-Drysdale 1987). Sometimes grown-ups feel they are expected to sit and talk with a child to demonstrate they are not colluding with him by, for instance, letting him play. At other times, there might be a tendency to collude and not confront the child through fear of his possible reaction. At these times, it is necessary that grown-ups can acknowledge their anxieties and support each other with the difficulty.

It is important to distinguish between an actual or natural consequence of an action or behavior and what we decide is consequence following the event. For instance, if a child breaks a window and people feel angry, the consequence of his action is that the window is broken and people are angry. With the most emotionally unintegrated children, the starting point for work is external reality. There is a range of possibilities in terms of what happens next. These will be related to the context of the particular event and general culture. For example, if there is a clear understanding that a house meeting is always called following an incident of hitting, then this would be one of the consequences.

Where we decide upon a particular response to a situation we need to be clear why we are doing it. In the case of the broken window, we could involve the child in clearing up the glass, replacing the window and paying towards the damage. If the damage was a regular occurrence, there could be consequences for the whole group about how the damage is to be paid for. The more integrated a child, the more we can expect him to be involved in working out which possibility is taken.

At times, we may feel a wish to bring in a particular consequence that a child will think or feel to be punitive. If a child is able to make reparation, he might actually feel relieved and positive that he can make reparation. Even if he is unable to make reparation, the experience that he has an impact felt by others to be of consequence could feel positive to him. The main problems would be if he felt he was of no consequence or if the consequences were overwhelming to him. These would confirm an underlying sense of being worthless and 'unsurvivable'.

A significant part of this work is to ensure that we let children know of the positive consequences of their behavior. We can do this by the way we respond to their positive gestures and contributions. Some children have difficulty facing and seeing the positive and constructive things they do, just as they do with actions that are more negative. Grown-ups need actually to show and explain this to a child. If our approach pays attention and acknowledges positive contributions then there will be greater potential for giving, repairing, and creating which provide alternatives and a balance to more difficult experiences.

How the staff team is able to work with each other on the consequences of their own behavior and interrelationships will set a tone for this whole area of work. Work with children can only go on in this sense once the grown-ups have a sound reality on which to base their own work.

Working through difficulties with children

How do we work with children when we think their behavior has been difficult? Following difficult episodes of behavior, we can have a strong urge to do something. At these times, we might also be under stress, and being clear of our motivation and aims is difficult. Often we say things to the child like, 'You need to talk to someone' or 'You need to sort something out with so-and-so.'

When we say things like this to a child, we may be letting him know that we have noticed through his behavior that he is struggling, that we are concerned about him and would like to talk with him so we can help him with the difficulty. We might also be setting down a boundary to let him know his behavior has gone over a limit. Sometimes, if we think a child has gone over a limit and we are feeling annoyed with him, telling him he is going to talk to someone and sort out his difficulties can seem punitive. This can be particularly so if we stop him from doing something else he wants to do. We should think carefully what our motives are at these times. It is likely children will have difficulty understanding their behavior and putting feelings into words. It might be better for us to put the emphasis on spending some time together, listening to the child and working something out together. Of course, if a child has gone over a limit we will need to let him know clearly it is not okay.

If a child is being disruptive, it is likely he is pushing out his difficult feelings to avoid something that is painful. Anyone who interrupts this could seem to him to be punitive and persecuting him, especially if the difficult feelings he is trying to get rid of are being returned to him. If an adult does stop a child then she will need to decide what to do next. For example, is it better to work with the situation straight away or come back to it once things have calmed down a bit? There is a risk if one is in an emotionally charged situation of using impersonal language, which children quickly recognize and use defensively. If we say things in a repetitive, unthinking way to children, it is likely they will do the same to explain things to us.

Sometimes it is useful to help a child think about his behavior and feelings, making links between things. At other times, we need to take responsibility for managing his environment so his frustration and anxiety are reduced, enabling him to forget his difficulties. Emotionally unintegrated children rapidly move in and out of different emotional states, especially when the environment around them changes in any way. They will need substantial emotional support to sustain any level of ego functioning.

At certain stages in a child's development, rather than ask him to talk or think about his difficulties, it is better that we try to hold the anxiety, so that he is able to get on. It may be better for him to get to the end of a day and feel his day has gone well without too many difficulties. While this might be illusory, it can also be a valuable experience for him to internalize. Working with a child in this way has to be balanced by a concern that we may be avoiding the work on difficulties by trying to get on with things.

If an adult is asked to be with a child and talk to him, it can feel as if she is expected to sort things out, so that the child does not carry on having difficulties. This pressure could be conveyed to the child by asking him to sort out his problems. Even if the child and adult are able to communicate, we cannot be sure the child's difficulties will not continue after this. Where a child does have difficulty following time with an adult, the adult can feel responsible as if she has failed in some way. The anxiety of not knowing and the uncertainty of what will happen next time can be demanding for us to deal with. To defend ourselves against this anxiety we may fantasize that we can find a reason for everything and that all situations can be resolved neatly. If we have unrealistic expectations of what we are able to understand and achieve, this might be passed onto children, for instance, by asking them to explain or think about things that are beyond their emotional capacity.

Authority

The authority of an adult working in a therapeutic way with a child is derived from the relationship and trust the child has in the adult. This type of authority is not static and is constantly changing according to the emotional climate of the relationship and therapeutic environment. Reflecting upon the nature of authority can give meaningful insights about individual relationships and the environment as a whole.

Although authority can be viewed in hierarchical terms according to the status of different individuals, in our work with children we are mainly working on the authority that develops through relationships. However, we may feel a dilemma between the need for a benign type of authority, developed over time, based on trust, and a more assertive authority that we might feel is needed to keep things under control. For example, if a group is unsafe, what type of authority is most likely to have an immediate impact? To what extent should we focus on matters of authority in our work with children and to what extent on authority between adults? In some cases, the lack of safety could be related to a sense that the team is not working effectively together. Whatever the underlying reasons may be, it is important that we do everything possible in the immediate sense to address serious breakdowns in authority and the crossing of boundaries.

The need to be in control can in itself lead to problems in authority and containment if it is driven too much by anxiety. For example, rather than the development of emotional holding through relationships, there can be an overreliance on holding in a concrete sense through physical holding and restraint. In some cases, it can seem that authority is equated with physical strength. In this type of culture, there could be an overreliance on role-based rather than personal authority. For a person to have authority, others must allow her to have it. Children allow us to have authority over them if they have gained trust in us through their experience of our responses to a whole range of situations. This is similar to the authority an infant may lend his mother through the experience of having his needs met by her repeatedly. This is the authority to provide something valued and needed, such as nurture, care and protection.

As well as authority coming from the work going on in individual relationships, children can also develop a sense of trust in adults through experiencing the adult in the wider context of the home. For example, a general sense of investment in the environment by adults, such as looking after the home, decorating and repairing things, may contribute to a feeling for children that adults can be trusted and given authority to care for them.

The way in which adults give each other permission to have authority will be one of the factors that children will pick up and respond to. Having authority can be perceived in terms of power and there may be a reluctance to share this in a team. If there is a feeling in a team that adults are reluctant to take authority, does this reflect a culture where people are not allowed to have authority? Again, this is most likely where authority is hierarchical and not personal. Hierarchical authority can be a defense against the anxieties involved in developing personal authority through emotional involvement.

Adults will need support to help manage and make sense of the anxieties involved in this work. The adult's capacity to keep a boundary and recognize the differences between inner and outer reality, me and not me, is central to the work. The more we are able to provide an appropriate sense of boundaries, the more a child may give us the authority to manage boundaries for them. This can feel like George Lyward's 'stern love' (Burn 1956), being clear about what is or is not okay, intervening when necessary to ensure appropriate boundaries are maintained and doing this out of concern for the child.

Where personal authority is missing or breaking down, teams can become immobilized or resort to using power. If power is going to be used it needs to be backed up by actual practical possibilities. For instance, if we say we are going to remove a child from a group, it is no use unless we know we can actually do it. The use of power in this way can be effective in the short term as long as the aim is clear and task-related, such as, to restore safety. This can be seen as taking authority and responsibility; knowing when this is needed contributes to the development of personal authority. If power is used in this way, space can also be given to restoring personal authority and relationships. An environment that relies purely on power is likely to be pushed into using increasingly extreme measures.

There is, at times, a conflict between authority and control. The development of personal authority and relationships does not necessarily lead to 'good' behavior. For example, if a child feels safe with an adult, he may also feel he can be difficult towards her. It might actually be a healthy development for some children that they become less compliant. If we think it is necessary to challenge the child's behavior, we need to be clear why and give him a sense of care rather than judgmental disapproval.

Our responses to children also take place within a wider environment and we may vary our responses according to the context we are in While we are helping children gradually distinguish between different contexts, we also need to be careful that our own anxieties are not passed onto children in a way that feels confusing. For example, if children swear a lot at home, they are not likely to stop because there is a visitor in the house. If we feel embarrassed that we do not appear in control and react strongly to the child, he could feel confused. If we do not normally respond like that and we disapprove so strongly, why do we normally let him do it? Are we more concerned about what the visitor might think than the child's actual behavior? It can be appropriate to respond to a child differently according to the situation as long as we are clear how and why we do this. In particular, we need to be attentive to how matters of authority can resonate with our own childhood and life experiences and become intertwined in our work.

Authority and containment in times of change

During times of change, there is often an atmosphere of uncertainty and heightened levels of anxiety which can make it difficult to contain children safely. The staff's and children's anxiety can feed into each other, creating a spiral effect. In work with traumatized children, the nature of authority between staff and children is central to safety and this in turn stems from the quality of relationships. Change can have a strong impact on our sense of authority and capacity to provide emotionally holding relationships.

A basic need in our work is safety. For an environment to be safe there needs to be a clear sense of authority provided by the adults. Effective authority will need an appropriate balance between attending to feelings and emotions, and providing authoritative direction. For example, it may be appropriate to consider children's and adult's feelings and views about something, and for this to influence any action taken. In another situation, it might be necessary to take a decision and then deal with how people feel about it and their views.

Safety can only be ensured partially by paying attention to concrete matters such as procedures and staff ratios. In our effort to ensure procedures are being followed and ratios of staff to children are adequate, it is essential we keep our focus on the importance of emotionally holding relationships. Given that our task is to provide a sense of security and stability for the children, uncertainty is demanding to work with. Due to external changes, there had been a feeling of a lack of safety in parts of the Community. Both children and adults were expressing this. There had been a high level of acting out by children and discontent expressed by staff over different matters. Morale felt low and at times staff seemed despondent. To some extent, this is consistent with a period of major change. We should think about what children and adults are actually saying, as well as asking why they are saying it at this particular time. Often in the past, significant change has been accompanied by higher staff turnover and breakdown in child placements. Changes of leadership have had a Community-wide impact, while changes of staff within house and education teams often have a specific impact on their groups. On the positive side now, staff turnover had not increased. This suggests that the difficult feelings and anxieties were being contained to some extent within the Community.

While we may be 'holding' difficulties within, it is also possible that we find an external focus for them. For example, a team or individual might focus on an external issue to avoid working on something closer to home. The external issue could feel safer, more within our control, and less threatening to think and talk about. This may seem particularly apparent if we find ourselves repeatedly focusing on the same external issue. At the same time, during periods of greater anxiety we might also be more alert and attentive to underlying difficulties. For example, if concerns about safety are heightened we may also be more concerned to address other concerns we have let drift.

The use of the word 'boundaries'

'Boundaries' was a word often used at the Cotswold Community and is used commonly in residential child care as well as in general society. 'Boundaries' is usually used in relation to limits and rules. The children referred had not developed a sense of their own personal boundaries so the word was also relevant to the boundary of the self and internal and external worlds. The different meanings of the word could confuse the way it was used.

Shapiro and Carr (1991), who look at child development within the family context, give a good sense of how personal boundaries develop.

> In essence, when parents ask their child, 'what is your experience?' they authorize the child to *have* a separate experience and allow an implicit boundary to form between child and parent. On one side of this boundary is the child's experience of himself; on the other side is the parents' views of him. This stable personal boundary constitutes a key element in healthy growth and development, since secure self-awareness allows the child to have flexible interactions with other people. (p.12)

Boundaries in this sense are quite different from rules, especially if those rules do not allow the child's experience of the rule to be acknowledged. Sometimes it seems that when we talk about establishing boundaries, we are more clearly talking about establishing rules that we shall all live by. We might avoid using the word 'rule' due to underlying anxieties, such as a worry of being punitive. The word 'boundary' is a form of jargon and not appropriate to use with children. It is much better to explain what we are doing and why, and to talk about that.

Chapter 10

Gender Issues, Sexuality and Dress

Due to their experiences, traumatized children often have a distorted perception of gender, for example, they might believe that men are violent and women submissive. In our work with traumatized children we have the opportunity to work through matters related to their own identity and gender, as well as to experience positive gender role models. Sexuality is closely associated with gender and the two may be confused for children who have been abused. We can expect traumatized children to have powerful feelings in relation to gender and sexuality and to be highly sensitized in this area. The way we dress expresses both our gender and sexuality, and needs careful consideration.

The gender balance in teams

In residential child care, it is probably unusual to find teams of staff equally balanced in terms of gender. Usually there are more female than male staff. At the Community, it was more usual to have more men than women.

Is it helpful in principle to aim for an equal balance and always to have at least one man and woman working? Sometimes when we are particularly anxious about the gender balance, we could give potentially negative messages to children – for example, if we say or imply, 'things won't be all right this evening unless there is a man working.' Some children become more panicky or violent when there is not a mix of men and women working.

It may be productive to work with a child's or adult's anxiety, rather than move things around in response to it.

How do we avoid reinforcing unhelpful assumptions about gender? What does a child need for his own development in terms of relationships with men and women? How relevant to a child are a person's qualities rather than their actual gender? For example, if only men or only women have worked with a child but with a balance of feminine and masculine qualities, how would this compare to both men and women working with the child?

Do we feel it is acceptable for women to have both 'maternal' and 'paternal' qualities? It seems more accepted for men to be both caring in a way associated with 'maternal' and aggressive as associated with 'paternal'. Do men take on the role of protecting women at work? If so, does this lead men to be more aggressive? Do we try to create or preserve an image of women as nurturing but nonaggressive and nonsexual?

The policy of not working with girls and some implications

As the Community deliberately excludes girls from being placed, the message is different from if their absence were coincidental. How different would our thoughts and feelings be about men working closely with young girls, as women do with boys? The absence of girls makes it difficult for teams to talk about and acknowledge the sexual aspects of work with children. It is difficult for men to talk of sexual dynamics between boys and men, as it can raise anxieties to do with their own sexuality. In this situation if women are more open about these dynamics, it could leave them vulnerable to dealing with all matters about sexuality. This creates a difficulty for the team in working with sexuality. However, the difficulty of introducing girls to the Community, how it may affect the treatment task and the additional difficulty in managing the relationships between boys and girls, are reasons why the Community continued to be boys only.

Dress and appearance in work

The question of what is an appropriate way of dressing is a complex one in therapeutic work with traumatized children. On the one hand, the aim is to provide a family type of environment not too removed from what is usual, but on the other hand, the group of children is highly traumatized and volatile, with a distorted experience of what is usual. We need to be clear about the message our appearance gives.

In our society, over the years different appearances have had different associations. For instance, the associations about men wearing earrings and women having tattoos have changed. The way we dress is significant. Dress and appearance can be a way of expressing one's identity and taking pleasure in this. This can also help children in finding their own identity and in valuing themselves. Children might copy the way adults and other children dress. This is not necessarily a problem and is normally how one moves towards an individual identity, by trying out various possibilities.

However, dress can be used in many other ways, consciously or unconsciously. For example:

- to excite, to cause envy, jealousy, rivalry, to seduce, to shock;
- to distance others, perhaps by overdressing;
- to create anxiety or a sense of being overwhelmed by looking run down or neglected.

These are, then, some simple considerations to bear in mind:

- How we dress and what we look like need to be appropriate to the work we do.
- Expressing one's self is potentially helpful to children.
- The way we dress should not make children feel excluded.
- Dress and appearance can be used in many ways, consciously or unconsciously, and need thinking about carefully.
- This issue crosses over many boundaries, for example, professional and personal.
- Matters of dress and appearance should be considered in relation to a person's cultural background, so that rules or guidelines are not discriminatory.

Dress and sexuality

Naturally, our style of dress portrays a sense of our sexuality. In work with children who have suffered physical and sexual abuse, our appearance can take on different meanings for the child, and can easily evoke strong feelings and anxiety. A culture developed in the Cotswold Community where men and women would dress similarly, typified by jeans, trainers and sweatshirt.

It is difficult at the Community for women to show their female side at work, as there is an anxiety that femininity may be sexually provocative. There is also a difficulty for men dressing how they would like to, for example, there has been an anxiety about earrings and tattoos because of negative associations with delinquency. What are our anxieties? How important to children is it that men and women can express their masculinity and femininity by the way they dress?

There could be a fear of women seducing or exciting children sexually. Is this a displacement of similar anxieties about men?

In early infant development, the mother is everything to the baby, though the baby is not everything to the mother. Do we desexualize ourselves to protect the children from adult's interest in each other, and to maintain the illusion we are only interested in them? If so, is this helpful and necessary?

Men wearing earrings at work

When the Community began in the late 1960s and early 1970s there were distinct dress codes, for example, men were not permitted to wear earrings. Partly, this was to avoid the negative associations of earrings that boys had. Now, it is more common for men to wear earrings and the notion that men should be permitted to do so was put forward in the Community, on the basis that the rule was outdated and unhelpful. While the issue of earrings may not now be a contemporary concern, the issue of body piercing is a continuing aspect of personal dress that will need acknowledging and working on with children and adults involved in this work.

From the 1960s to the early 1990s men were not allowed to wear earrings at work in the Community and nor were children in primary houses, while children in the secondary house could wear them in the house but not school. When these rules were made, there was particular concern about the delinquent association that went with men wearing earrings and the way children in approved schools and other similar environments often viewed ear piercing or tattoos as a delinquent code. There could also be other issues, such as the blurring of sexual difference and practical matters related to safety.

Different people have different associations towards the issue of earrings, though overall the issues are quite different from what they were 20 or 30 years ago. The delinquent association no longer seems so relevant. If men wear earrings, boys might be more likely to want to do so, possibly through wanting to identify with them. If a child wants to wear an earring, should we let him and will all children want to do the same? In primary houses, we should either let things stay as they are for children, or look at each case individually as it arises. If we did think of letting a child wear an earring, we would need to discuss that with his parents or social worker, seeking their involvement and advice.

Whether this kind of change is useful or a hindrance to the work with children will largely depend upon how these matters are approached. There is potential value in working through some of the concerns involved. There are anxieties about body piercing and what it may represent, in particular to children who have been traumatized and abused. We should be attentive to this when thinking about the feelings of individual children.

If the rule about earrings is moved, more matters might arise about other forms of body piercing. Some of these matters are more complex and include cultural differences. A key issue in our approach to what we decide is whether the impact of the decision will be helpful or not in the work of treating traumatized children.

The provision of sex education for emotionally unintegrated children

Providing sex education is a difficult parental task in ordinary childhood. Where children are traumatized, emotionally held back and possibly sexually abused, it is additionally difficult. However, this work is essential for these vulnerable children.

How do we know when to start? There is no definite starting time. It will be a combination of a child's behavior and an assessment from the people who know and work with him that will determine the need for this work. It will be a similar process in deciding when to end the work.

Any worker undertaking the work of providing sex education will need to be in a 'parental' role as opposed to that of therapist, that is, the concerned 'parent' providing straightforward information, rather than the therapist working with the inner world.

Although the main aim of this work is not working with sexual abuse but sexual information for the unintegrated child, it will undoubtedly have a bearing on the former as a high percentage of the children we work with have been sexually abused.

Beginning the work

In an ideal world, one would wait to be approached by the child and be guided by him, following his lead. However, to wait for the child to ask questions about sex might never happen and would certainly be the easy option. The fact remains we have growing sexual beings before us (many of them reaching puberty) and we have a responsibility, as possibly the only caring role models they have at the moment, to equip them in the best way possible to deal with life and negotiate relationships.

For the worker entering into this with a child, there are a number of matters to address before the work begins. The workers involved will need to feel comfortable with their own knowledge and feelings of sex and sexuality. Some self-awareness will certainly be necessary. One's sexuality and gender will be of significant importance. Am I a sexual being? Where do I fit within the scheme of sexual relationships? How do I feel about the child's newly emerging sexuality?

The workers undertaking this work will need to use the team they work in, both in team meetings and team consultancies, to talk about sexual matters and to focus on preparing themselves for the types of questions and likely areas of anxiety that might surface. They will need to think together about how to respond, and to express their own feelings about being asked questions on this intimate subject.

Creating some ground rules at the beginning of the work will help establish the boundaries that, in turn, will help manage anxiety. It may not be necessary to map these out for the child but they are useful for the worker to hold in mind. For instance, it is okay to ask questions, though personal questions should not be answered. It is okay to feel embarrassed.

Where the work takes place with each child should be thought about carefully, bearing in mind the safety of the situation and the various associations that might exist. However, clearly the child's bedroom should not be used. Past associations may be reawakened and it could feel as if the child's personal space is being invaded.

Who should undertake the work? A female or male worker? Should it be one worker or would two workers be the better option? If so, would it be one of either sex? It is necessary to think carefully about the anxieties connected with these matters for both children and adults before making decisions on which way to go forward.

It is paramount that the worker involved has a supervisor and time to reflect on the work, enabling them to discuss and explore the issues that have arisen.

Approach to the work

The approach to the work will vary from child to child. The needs of each child will have to be carefully assessed. For instance, do we have one session following in a planned way to the next? Should it be left freer to take the lead from the children? Perhaps striking some form of balance between the various approaches will determine a way forward.

One should avoid using words such as 'natural', 'normal' and 'nice', which may be meaningless to the child, or contradictory to his experience, leaving him feeling misunderstood. Our notions of sex and sexuality, care and loving relationships could be quite unreal to the child given his previous experience.

The information provided needs to be pitched at the right level for the individual involved. It is important not to teach too much as information can suppress fantasy. This imaginative, unconscious activity might provide some indication of the child's inner world and enable the child to eventually reach some self-awareness and understanding. The worker involved in the parental role is not in a position to work within this fantasy, but another team member in the role of therapist may be able to do so.

The worker will need to bear in mind that the child's previous experience of talking about sex with an adult might have been the prelude to actual physical experience and to be aware that this could be what the child is anticipating. It is essential that the workers do not see the child's behavior and experience as perversion and lose sight of the whole child, seeing only the abuse.

Supervision and the involvement of others outside of the individual work

Space in team meetings and team consultancies can be a forum to discuss what this work involves. It can be productive to acknowledge and try to understand any feelings brought up, such as embarrassment. Team involvement is also necessary to avoid creating a relationship where a child and worker feel split off and isolated from the group, which can feel unsafe and possibly reflect the child's previous experience.

The concepts of transference, countertransference and projection are necessary and useful tools for the worker. They can help in understanding how the child is feeling and experiencing the situation and what he might have experienced in the past.

The workers involved need to work on their own feelings aroused by talking about sex. This should be discussed in supervision.

Before beginning this work, we should discuss it with the social worker and parents if this is appropriate. This will enable them to know what is happening and will also help prevent a situation developing that feels secretive or split off from others, possibly echoing the child's previous experience. At the same time, this needs to be done sensitively to protect the child's fragile sense of personal boundaries.

Children's sexuality and involvement with each other

In ordinary development, children often explore their sexuality with each other, for example, through play and games. However, for vulnerable children who have experienced abuse and who are in care this is a complex area. It is difficult to get the right balance between providing appropriate protection and being over protective in an oppressive way. There was a period at the Community when there had been a number of instances of sexual involvement between children and we were struggling with achieving this balance.

We should have a framework for thinking about the issues. Where there is specific sexual involvement between children there could be questions regarding the direct management of those situations. For example, do we need to manage things differently to reduce the opportunities children have for sexual involvement with each other? Is part of the problem that the times when children become involved with each other are not managed or dealt with in a way that creates a feeling of safety? Do we need to work with children more directly about their involvement with each other, emphasizing the importance of personal safety and space, and what is and is not okay?

An example of an intervention related to the above could involve using a system to check where children are during the night. Another approach could be to focus on the issue of sexuality in general. Does the involvement between children reflect needs that children have in this area that are not being noticed and dealt with by the adults? For example, are there children who are confused about sex and their sexuality and who need more individual attention? This could be mainly to help work on their specific difficulties and experiences, but could also be a form of sex education. An example of this approach could be to set up a series of individual meetings so that the child can work on sex and sexuality. It is important in this work not to impose our own cultural values and experiences in the way we talk about sex.

A third approach is to consider the sexual involvement between children as the manifestation or symptom of a wider issue, which may or may not be specifically sexual. An example could be the loss of boundaries in general, which might lead to the blurring of physical boundaries between people. Supervision is a useful forum for adults to maintain a sense of their own boundaries by working through things, distinguishing between me and not me, internal and external reality. If the boundary of supervision is inadequate, adults might lose a sense of boundaries, which could then make it difficult to set boundaries for children. In this case, the approach to the problem will be to reestablish boundaries in general. Changes in routine could actually be unhelpful, as children might perceive it as another boundary being lost and it could provoke an anxious reaction, which could then further reduce the sense of safety.

Within this framework, there are many different things to think about. If children are seeking physical contact with each other, it may be that adults are felt to be physically unapproachable and the only avenue open for exploration is with each other. Children are often curious about their parents' bodies and learn through actual physical contact, sometimes by showing their own bodies to parents. It is noticeable on group holidays with children or on swimming trips how interested a child may be in looking at an adult's body, for example, some children seem fascinated in watching men shave. These ordinary types of experiences are not open to children in day-to-day life in residential homes.

The anxieties we have with physical contact can complicate things further. Some of this is fuelled by child protection anxieties, which can sexualize things in a negative way. For instance, we might be more likely to use a phrase like 'exposed himself' rather than showed himself. The word 'abuse' is powerful and suggests a degree of control and intent, which does not fit with the more impulsive and panicky behavior of emotionally unintegrated children. At what point in normal child development would we think a child capable of being abusive? We need to distinguish more between what feels and what actually is abusive.

It is important that we work on these difficulties and try to provide children with appropriate opportunities for excitement, love and affection. Our aim should be to create a culture that is life-affirming, exciting and interesting. This type of culture is safe in the sense that it is potentially containing. Where we seem unable to create a safe culture there are dilemmas in how to provide protection for the group as a whole. It might be helpful to think of all those in the group as potential victims, rather than to focus on one child as the 'abuser' or bully and others as victims. The 'abuser's' behavior is also destructive to himself and could be the result of feeling unsafe. There could be a point where it feels impossible to continue with the risks involved, and removing a child from the group is necessary. If this happens we need to be careful in managing the situation so we are clear about our responsibility and the child's. With children who are more unintegrated, we can put the emphasis on our decision to remove him so that he and the other children might be safer.

Insufficient emotional involvement from the adults could be connected to children seeking involvement with each other as a form of self-provision, or as a lack of appropriate management from adults. This may show itself, for instance, by an increase in the number of incidents and accidents. Children might comment on how tired some adults look. Are we clearly focused on children's needs and directing them to the appropriate adults for care?

Another possibility is that matters that belong with the adult team but are not being acknowledged are picked up unconsciously by the children and are enacted by them. This could be anxiety the adults have about sexuality and their relationships with each other. It could be connected to external events that are affecting the adults. For instance, media coverage of news events is often pervasive and sexually explicit. The nature of the news, as well as drawing attention to sex, also raises matters related to authority, trust, deceit, being caught and guilt. The type of anxieties potentially raised by these matters could lead to defensiveness in adults which might affect their capacity to work in these areas with children.

Chapter 11

Working with Absence and Break Periods

Therapeutic work with traumatized children will involve work on what is absent, missing and lost. For example, the absent parent or the move away from home, or in some cases many moves from many homes. Whenever there is an experience of absence or a break in our work with traumatized children, we can expect to work with it in terms of the here and now, as well as in the context of the past. Therefore, absences and breaks provide difficulties to work through in the present, which are compounded by the child's past. This can make absences and breaks seem like an unhelpful disruption to treatment. However, as trauma is often associated with absences and breaks, working through these issues with the child is part of the recovery from trauma.

The Cotswold Community worked on sessions lasting a school term, with the children returning to birth or foster parents for break periods (school holidays). This meant that there were regular breaks, with endings and beginnings. This was how the Community was established in the 1960s and once this was established it was not an easy structure to change, for example to a 52-weeks-a-year home. Often it felt as if we were merely enduring this structure and the comings and goings with all the difficulties involved for an emotionally fragile group of children. On reflection, after 30 years of working in this way it seemed possible that the work around absences and breaks was a key factor in the children's recovery.

Going away for break periods

Working with children on the basis that they would spend holiday or break periods at home with their birth or foster family was an expectation at the beginning of the child's placement and if a family placement did not exist at this point, the aim would be to establish one as soon as possible. The break periods were shorter than the normal school holidays and when necessary children could spend less time away, so that their treatment would not be too disrupted at critical times and so that the time away could be a positive experience. If necessary, staff would also provide support to the child and family during the break period. Inevitably, the ending of terms and the beginning of new ones were demanding and often fraught times.

The reason we have breaks could be viewed as a practical necessity to enable staff to take holiday. If breaks really are counterproductive to treatment, another model could be a 52-weeks-a-year placement, with children's and adults' time away being planned individually throughout the year. However, this current structure is central to the therapeutic approach.

Children are provided with an experience that is representative of early primary care, of which they have been deprived. The Community takes on a role similar to that provided by a parent for her infant, involving a high level of dependency. The difference for children in the Community compared with infants and their parents is that the provision is representative of early experience and has an illusory 'as if' quality – the Community can never really be a child's parent or family. There need to be times when a child can believe the illusion, normally as part of a localized regression. Having break periods helps to keep this distinction established. The distinction is partly to do with having somewhere outside of the Community, ideally a family that the child feels part of and where there is a long-term future. The experience in the Community is intense with a specific therapeutic focus, so the breaks also help to give children a change from this and an experience that is more based on normality.

There could be occasions when we feel it is too disruptive to a child's treatment for him to go away from the Community, for example, a child with an unsuitable break placement or one who has only just arrived. In these cases, there might be reasons why it could be beneficial for a child to stay. While there are a few children who do stay for these reasons, most children stay because they have nowhere else to go. If there were an intensive primary care house, it would be easier for it to be an appropriate part of the culture for a child to stay in the break. The reasons could be clearly connected to his treatment and being part of that house. He would not feel as different and excluded as a child who lives in a house where most other children go away for breaks.

Work with children during break periods

During the break periods, staff would work with those children remaining in the Community and arrange contact for those who were away with families.

We have break periods for the following reasons:

- to help ensure that the child's treatment is localized;
- to help prevent institutionalization;
- as a break from the intensity of treatment;
- as an experience of life outside the Community to which children will be returning;
- a family is something to look and move towards;
- a sense of still being connected and belonging to a family is important in our culture;
- an experience of external reality, which a child can test himself against;
- an opportunity for the child and family to acknowledge and adjust to changes that take place for them;
- a practical way of arranging breaks away for children and adults;
- a chance for adults to recover, recharge and enjoy.

Reasons such as these are less relevant for some of the children. Emotionally unintegrated or frozen (Dockar-Drysdale 1958) children first need to become established in a dependant attachment before they can begin to experience a sense of boundaries and separation. For these children, breaks may reinforce their chameleon-like capacity to adapt to or merge with whatever environment they are in. They might benefit from more continuity until a relationship has been established.

Break periods raise certain feelings and issues, such as:

- a sense of continually stopping and starting, especially when sessions (terms) are short. It is difficult to focus on being here during a short session. On the other hand, a short session can feel more manageable and less exhausting;
- a loss and interruption of our contact with children and daily routines;
- excitement, hope, anxiety, worries about the break – for the children and us;

- fear of complaints from parents about us and rivalry between parents and us;
- feelings of rejection and abandonment, and anger or guilt connected with these feelings;
- relief, tiredness and a sense of collapse;
- feelings about beginning a new session, both hopeful and fearful.

Some of these feelings are more difficult to acknowledge than others. For instance, relief may be easier to express than sadness. Work at these times can be similar to mourning. Within this context, working with children who are here in the break is a difficult task. Often the reasons children stay here for breaks are difficult and sometimes traumatic rather than as part of a treatment plan, for example, because of a family placement breakdown. The sense of being rejected, abandoned and unlovable is powerful. The fact that the majority of children go away can reinforce these feelings. Working with these children requires us to deal with what is felt about going away and to contain potentially powerful feelings for the children who remain. Children going away could feel angry with us for 'kicking them out', while the children here might feel angry with us for not letting them have anywhere to go. It is difficult to know the best way of dealing with this. How can we provide a break from treatment, while still allowing children to communicate their real feelings about being here? Similarly, how do staff communicate with each other during breaks?

We often think of breaks as an interruption to treatment but as they are such a significant and constant part of the culture, it could be argued they are integral to the therapeutic process. We have mentioned some of the potential benefits of a family break placement. As well as these, the break periods provide a structured focus for working on and reworking issues connected with endings and beginnings. These issues are central to growth and development.

Support for children who are away for break periods

An approach of supporting children when away with their family could include visiting the child at home with his family, sending postcards and making phone calls. Though the explicit aim is to support the child and his family, so that the break can be successfully sustained, a key aim of the break period is to provide the child with an experience of separation.

We have a clear expectation that children are away for the whole break period, though a child could stay at the home if necessary for his treatment – for example, being in a regression which should not be disrupted. Mainly, children actually stay because they have no break placement, or the placement can only manage a few days.

For children who are away, contact should be planned for each child during the break by telephone, postcards and visits, and he should know this before the break. This is to help bridge the gap between one session (term) and the next, and to give the child a sense of being in our thoughts and minds, rather than being abandoned.

There are questions to be asked about a break. How much of our work during the break is supporting his family or carers and how much the child? Some parents find it useful to talk to adults here if things are difficult. We should focus in this work on asking the parents what they find helpful in our contact with them and what they would like us to do. The idea of support can feel undermining to some parents, so the emphasis should be on how we can best work together on a child's break. Sometimes parents do not find it helpful for us to send postcards or ring unexpectedly. If we do feel a child needs contact from us, this should be discussed with the parents so that they do not feel undermined. We should think carefully about the sense a child is likely to make of any contact or lack of it. A child could need a clear break from the intensity of his treatment and keeping in touch with him may prevent this from happening. We should also acknowledge and talk about our own anxieties connected to break periods, being away from the children and children going away. If we do not think about this, our contact could be driven by our own anxieties rather than a child's need.

It can be helpful to see the child's home and meet his parents there. We could take the child to visit during the session. It might help him if we look at his home together and for him to see his parents and us together. It is also beneficial for the child to know that we talk and think about him before and after breaks and that this kind of relationship and communication goes on throughout the year. Communication about the break helps us put things into a context, though a child's emotional experience may be quite different from what is described.

Sometimes visits during the break can become ritualized. For instance, a trip to the cinema followed by a McDonald's can become an expected 'goody'. Again, the parents might feel that this undermines them, in view of what they are trying to provide. The emphasis on 'goodies' can also become a feature for children staying during the breaks.

Working with the impact of staff illness and absence

This is a perennial difficulty in residential child care and due to the stress involved there is a tendency to respond in a practical way with the emphasis on covering the gap. It is useful to try to think about what is involved to overcome it. In this way, the absence can be an opportunity in therapeutic work with the children and not just a nuisance.

Concern was expressed about the effect staff illness was having on the children. We decided to think about our own feelings when other adults are away ill. How do different people view it? How do staff feel about being ill and away from work? What is it like to be in a team coping with absence? How do children experience the absence?

At a fantasy level, there may be anxieties about the absence. Is the person ill because the work, the children or the team are too much or too difficult? Anxiety that destructive feelings are unmanageable might increase. The absence could seem like a rejection or abandonment. The children and adults might feel let down and angry with the absent person. Staff may feel left with it, having to work harder and so possibly may feel resentful. A sense can prevail that the option of being ill has been taken away from those left to soldier on. There might be envy towards the absent adult, because she is away from the difficulties at work and because she has allowed herself to be ill. If we find it difficult to acknowledge our own vulnerability or show it, envy can show itself in contempt towards the person ill. It may be believed that the person is not ill. Children are often quick to voice the anxiety that the person is dead or will not be coming back. There may be worry and concern for the person ill – why is she ill? Will she get better? Have we made her ill?

There could be a heightened sense that things could get worse – who is going to be ill next? Children might feel more panicky and fearful of disintegration. Each child will need thinking about in terms of his own treatment needs. Absence will have different implications depending on the absent person's role. Often covering absence requires a team (and children) to stretch themselves. If structures such as supervision and training become unreliable at the same time, work can begin to feel like a matter of survival. If the team starts to feel this, then concern for each other, the children and the absent person soon falls. Sometimes angry feelings are acted out towards the children and among the staff team. At other times, the staff and children might draw together as a protest against the absent person. Both of these are defenses against acknowledging and working with the range of feelings in such a situation.

On a practical level, some things need rearranging to make sure they still happen and some things will not happen and will be missed. In the short term, these practical changes are temporary and transient, but in the longer term, they may feel like a real change. This kind of change can create anxiety and be harder work when the absence ends. The more emotionally unintegrated children will need reliable plans made to cover the absence. Children who are more integrated may need help to feel the absence, express feelings about it and think about it. Absence in itself is not necessarily a bad experience in a child's treatment. If the feelings involved can be managed and worked with, the absence also has the potential for growth in it – for example, by helping him to manage separation and deal with feelings of loss. Children may be able to think about the gap, the absent person and their relationship with her.

If the absence is longer, thinking can become more difficult. This raises the question of how a team keeps the image of a person alive during absence and the importance of contact where appropriate. Some contact between the absent staff member and the house, especially the children for whom she is responsible, is important. We should have an expectation of being in some kind of contact with the house. Even if the contact is by means of another staff member, it can feel that they are in touch. It can also be a positive experience for children to see adults thinking about their colleague. Sometimes children like to help make a get well card.

The absent staff member might also have difficulties, feelings and anxieties that mirror most of those mentioned. The staff member's return to work may also be difficult to deal with. It might feel easier to breathe a sigh of relief and deny the difficulties rather than work with them. There may be different responses such as 'Good to see you back' or 'Now you can do your bit' or 'No wonder children get angry with you.' The person returning to work may also have ambivalent feelings that need working with. The team needs to tackle this so they are able to help the children with what they are feeling.

Staff meetings and matters related to absence

When meetings have irregular attendance and timekeeping is poor, it can be useful to question whether underlying factors are contributing to this. When this happened at the Community we explored the reasons why and the issues involved. Some of the absence had been due to illness but most of it has been due to the need for cover in houses. This had not tended to be such a problem in the past.

The group can feel undervalued when attendance is inconsistent; this can also feel as if the functioning of the group is under attack. Ambivalence in relation to the task of the group can arise both from within and without the group. If group members are feeling more ambivalent about the group, they are more likely to take rather than resist opportunities to be absent. Sometimes crises with children can be used to avoid other difficulties and children may respond to our anxieties by providing us with opportunities for deflection. The group members' response to the absence will depend partly on how they feel about the group.

In the case of the particular time at the Community, it had been a hard session stretching our capacity to contain disturbance and hold boundaries. There seemed to have been a lot of staff illness. If a house is generally struggling in its work with children, the home manager and senior practitioner (therapeutic resource) might be held responsible in a way that seems punitive. These factors may have contributed to some of the difficulties in attendance.

It was suggested that the death through illness of one of our children might also be a factor. Following a death, it can be uncomfortable to be in a group. Some staff have found groups, such as team meetings and consultancies, very difficult. Following the child's death what were the expectations of the therapeutic resource group? The death of a child may challenge our belief in our capacity to nurture and there may be an underlying sense of failure. Following a death there can be an inhibition to talk about it. Many different anxieties are close to the surface. It can also seem trivial to talk about anything else. We felt we needed to come to terms with what happened before we could discuss this as a group. Powerful feelings have been close to the surface and difficult to think about.

Staff attendance on external courses and the implications for treatment

It is widely recognized that residential child care staff receive little training. On occasions where staff are out training, children may become more difficult and there is a danger of reacting to this by calling the staff back.

The attendance on external training courses during work time raises many treatment-related matters. A common theme is the feeling that children are being deprived of the absent adult's time. This will be especially so where there is an underlying assumption that the more time a child has with his carer, the better this will be for his treatment. When the Community reduced hours of work, there was a concern that children's treatment would suffer if we reduced them any further. To help ensure children experience a high level of continuity, there are clear guidelines providing a framework for organizing cover. As well as concern about the amount of time spent with children, we need to balance this with quality, which will be closely connected with staff development and training.

Staff may be envious about the course and resentful about covering for the absence. Often the staff member on the course is treated as if she is having a day off or having an easy time. For her part, it might seem difficult to share the experience with the team and for the team to show any curiosity or interest in it.

If someone is attending an external course, children may experience thoughts and feelings about separation. Going away from the workplace is more likely to do this than attending training and other events in house. Going out raises curiosity, interest and possible excitement about what is outside. It can also raise feelings connected to abandonment or taking flight. For example, children have said things to adults going on courses like, 'I bet you're going to raves' or 'You don't care anymore.'

If one team member is going out to a course, it may cause other team members to think about something similar. For some adults this may just take the form of getting more in touch with their own interests and desires. There is a balance between involvement with children and their internal worlds and maintaining one's sense of self externally to this. This balance enables children to experience emotional containment, but also the opportunity to move towards something that is not in their immediate world, making them curious. The balance will vary according to where different children are in their individual treatment. For instance, emotionally unintegrated children have a need to feel they are the centre of attention.

A child's carer leaving him something when she goes

The approach to meeting the needs of emotionally unintegrated children placed great importance on the establishment of a primary attachment between a child and his focal-carer, within which the child could receive primary provision. This level of dependency required the adult to be literally available and present for significant periods. Staff worked long hours, about 70 a week. To help establish and sustain a dependency it was felt there needed to be a way of holding the child emotionally during the focal-carer's absence. An approach developed whereby each child had a clearly designated back-up carer during this time and the carer would leave something for the child such as a postcard, which would normally be given to him by the back-up carer at bedtime. This was beneficial for some children, but we felt that we needed to reconsider the purpose behind the practice.

When a child arrives he may have no sense of being cared for, or that anyone thinks about him. Hence the system of leaving something like a postcard in the focal-carer's absence helps to show him he is not forgotten. This can be given to him by the back-up carer and can help to establish the idea for the child that his carer's absence does not mean he is forgotten. In the early stages of a relationship, it could be a way of reminding the child of the carer's absence in a concrete way.

It is acceptable if a child asks his carer to leave something, perhaps a personal item of her own, and this does not complicate matters. A child might find an object that he already has (a teddy or a piece of clothing) and use this to help during the absence. However, there is no general rule and the needs of each child should be assessed individually. It is important not to buy or leave anything special that may suggest compensating for the absence, or which prevents the child from expressing his difficult feelings or relieves any guilt and anxiety the adult feels about going.

Once a child has become emotionally dependant on his carer and there is a sense of being thought about and cared for, it is better to work with the feelings about the carer being absent and not try to fill this gap. The carer and other adults can show their awareness of the difficulty and talk and think about it with him. Ideally, if the child has been left something this should stop when the child decides for himself that he no longer needs it.

Chapter 12

Leavings, Endings and Beginnings

Traumatized children are likely to have experienced difficult endings and leavings. Trauma disrupts the sense of self. Rather than experiences having a beginning, middle and end, the trauma disrupts the ending or becomes the end. Traumatized children often find it difficult to complete or enjoy experiences due to their fear of what is coming next. Trauma may have been followed by changes and endings in the child's life such as leaving home. Endings or leavings might have been followed by trauma. The careful management of leavings, whether it is the child or an adult who is leaving, provides the opportunity for addressing many matters connected with trauma.

Preparation for a child's planned leaving

For anyone, leaving home can be difficult. It is especially so for a young person who is leaving a residential home, where he may have been living for many years but may have no continuing support and contact that a family might provide. It is crucial to prepare for this so that the transition is positive.

During a child's treatment, the sense that he is ready to leave may come from him, those working with him, his parents or social worker. When this question arises, it will need to be discussed. There is a need for a clear procedure to assess the appropriateness of leaving. The potential to collude in the ending of a child's placement comes from all directions. The child may invite us to collude with him, avoiding his real needs by presenting as a pseudomature personality, or to deny his development by behaving difficultly. He may show us what we knew to be his biggest difficulties to hide the progress he has made. We might want to keep a child because it feels better than having to start again with a new child. We could keep him to avoid our anxieties about the child's need to grow up, the need for a 'proper' education and fears that he would not cope outside.

If it is decided he is ready to leave, what work should go on to prepare him for that? The therapeutic task is to help the child build up and consolidate his inner resources, which he will need to manage his life and relationships with other people. Preparation for this within his treatment would include working on the separation involved and helping him to think about working things out for himself. Children may wonder how to work things out and may ask questions. Some children might defend themselves by not worrying or wanting to know how to do things. We should respond to a child's wish to understand and know about things, but not impose too much of what we think he should know about. It will help his development to find things out for himself and learn from experience.

Our role when we act as parents or therapists is confusing. Children are separating from a therapeutic relationship. If we take a pure treatment model, an ending would be quite clear and planned in advance. We would prepare about the feelings involved. If we take a normal family situation, hopefully there would be some work on feelings, maybe some practical preparation and continuing support. However, it would be misleading to think all young people leave home with skills such as knowing how to cook and budget. Learning is often by trial and error.

When a child is leaving, there could be many feelings for all involved, such as sadness, worry, anxiety, envy, jealousy, identification and anger. These need thinking about and acknowledging, so that they do not affect the child too adversely. We should plan future contact with a child according to his needs, in discussion with him, the team, his parents and social worker. This should not be left up to him and we should formally record what is agreed, so contact and support are not left to chance.

Marking a child's leaving from a house

When a child leaves his residential home, this is a significant event in his life and for the staff and the other children. Finding an appropriate way of marking these events is a key part of developing the culture of the home.

It is part of the culture to mark a child's leaving from a house with a group gathering, as well as to do things individually with the child. This also happens when a child leaves a school group and when an adult leaves.

Normally the group of children and adults gather together with the child, talk and think about his time here, the ending, the future, and give the child a gift. Sometimes children will acknowledge the leaving in their own way by saying something or giving a gift. These occasions have a sense of ceremony and ritual about them. But can this become a bit sterile if it is always the same, and what should happen if a child who is leaving does not want to be involved?

Ceremonies and rituals connected to significant life events such as marriage and death combine predictability and uniqueness. Partly this can provide a containing function at times of change and uncertainty. To know that something predictable will happen at these times may provide a sense of security. There might be some security in knowing what kind of leaving can be expected before it happens. Fears of being abandoned, rejected and forgotten about could be heightened if there is no idea how the leaving would be marked. At the same time, each leaving is individual, special and unique.

If these occasions are dull, it might be an enactment of loss and something dying. It could represent a lack of investment or refusal to acknowledge the ending and become involved with feelings of loss. Similarly, a focus on activity and doing things to mark the ending could also be a distraction and avoidance of those feelings. Neither dullness nor excitement are in themselves inappropriate to leavings; it may just help our understanding to question what these feelings represent at these times. The leaving is about those left behind as well as the one leaving. If the child leaving finds it too difficult to be involved with the group, the group gathering can still happen to mark the leaving. The child can have individual support while this is happening. It is important for there to be a time together, especially to think and talk about what is happening.

Are there underlying factors making it particularly difficult for us to think about leavings? Most of the adult and child leavings are bunched together at this time. It might be difficult to think about leavings other than those that have immediate relevance. The change in emphasis in the reasons for a child's leaving will also have had an impact. More leavings seem to be connected with funding and education rather than on overall development. If a leaving happens purely because a child is ready to leave, then a significant milestone has been arrived at. Marking this moment with a special event is necessary. It is not so easy to do this if the leaving seems arbitrarily imposed. It may not feel like a real ending.

Special trip out provided for a child by an adult who is leaving

An adult leaving a house would take out a child for whom she was the carer, for a special trip as a way of marking her time with the child. It was necessary to discuss why and what we hoped to achieve.

There were a number of questions to think about:

- Does the special trip make it more difficult for the child to express his feelings about the adult leaving?
- Does it make the child feel guilty about any anger he might have towards the adult?
- Does offering the trip ease feelings of guilt the adult may have about leaving?
- Does the emphasis on enjoying the trip make it difficult to experience loss?

It is important to mark an adult's leaving to emphasize the reality of the leaving. This should involve the group and individuals. It could be as simple as saying farewells. The farewell will probably be most meaningful if it is within the context of something the child and adult normally do together.

The continuing contact with a child after he leaves a house

Often when a child leaves a residential home, continuing contact with the home can be patchy and unreliable. The child leaving the home has a need for such contact in the same way a child leaving a family has. Providing this can be difficult and complex.

There are two ways in which a child leaves. One is where a child moves to the secondary house from a primary house, the other is where he leaves the Community. In both areas, we have a clear idea of the work we need to do (see 'Preparation for a child's planned leaving' above). However, in practice, whatever we may intend, it seems difficult actually to make plans and carry them out. As a result, often children leaving a house experience a sharp cutoff and little contact with the staff who have been significant to them.

Some of the anxieties that probably lie beneath this difficulty are:

- guilt about the child leaving – a feeling that we have got rid of him;
- relief that he has gone, especially if the leaving has been hard work;

- anger towards the child for leaving us, for not fully appreciating everything we have done for him;
- one child leaving often means beginning again with another – back to square one again;
- a wish to forget everything that has been gone through;
- sadness and a sense of loss;
- concern for the child and his future (Will he be all right? Will he want to see us again?);
- not wanting to get in the way and tread on the toes of the people he is with now;
- concern that he will like them more than us; they may do better for him (Will we hold him back by not letting go properly?);
- wondering whether we have time to spend keeping in contact when we have more pressing needs to meet.

Each leaving can bring with it its own anxieties. The child and the people he is going to live with will also have equally powerful feelings. Given the difficulty involved, it is clear that without careful work the safest option might be to do nothing. In some cases, the child may actually benefit more from a sense of someone being there for him when he needs it, rather than regular planned contact. In other cases, the child might need regular contact. The need for contact will be different for each child according to his circumstances, the nature of his relationships and his development. The nature of the contact needs to be discussed with the child and in the staff team, so that it is conscious and planned rather than left to chance.

When a child and adult have contact, it can feel awkward to know what to say or do. The child may be quite dismissive and disparaging about the adult. It is better to face these anxieties and make them more real rather than try to avoid them by not having contact. The child could be relieved that the contact and concern for him continues despite the difficulty. As mentioned earlier he will have many anxieties of his own, for example, that people are glad that he is gone, or he is so difficult that no one will want to see him again.

Future contact with an adult who has left

When an adult leaves, she, the children and other adults will all have feelings and opinions about the future contact they would like. Leaving will raise feelings and anxieties about separation, loss, rejection and abandonment.

Talking and thinking about this may enable a level of contact to be arranged that is right for all concerned. We recommend that the team manager organizes this, working towards a clear understanding of future contact before the adult leaves. A clear agreement about the future contact can help reduce anxieties for everyone.

Working with a carer's leaving and the care of individual children during this change

Due to the disruptions and number of different placements the children we work with have experienced, we attempt to provide a level of care that feels highly consistent and reliable. When staff who are working with the child decide to leave, it can feel as if we are recreating the child's past experiences of disruption. How we care for children during these changes needs careful thought.

The model of care provided in the Community focused on the one-to-one relationship between child and carer. This relationship can then develop into a key part of a child's treatment. We try to ensure that this relationship is as reliable as possible. However, there are inevitable difficulties involved in organizing this. For instance, an adult who is leaving in six months may also be the carer for only one child. The group might not yet know about the leaving. In the six-month period before she leaves, should she become focal-carer for a new child? If this adult takes on the new child, should he be told about her leaving? If he is told, will this hold him back from making attachments? If he is not told straight away, how may he be affected when he hears about it later?

When an adult has decided to leave, how do we decide when to tell the children? On the one hand, passing on the news makes it seem concrete and known about. However, it could also be argued that once a clear decision is made in the adult's mind, this will be communicated nonverbally. Once an adult has decided to leave, she is likely to behave differently in some way, and this could be picked up consciously or unconsciously. This may be particularly unhelpful to children who are testing their perception of reality and not able to make sense of what they are told is happening. For instance, a child might actually ask the adult if she is leaving and be told no. To give a child the information at this point can help him make sense of feelings he is picking up but of which he is unsure. At times, children need protecting from aspects of reality. However, when it is something so fundamental to us and the work with children, this might not be possible.

In relation to leavings and endings a key question is, can we work with the children and contain the feelings involved? Leavings should be announced with the longest possible time to deal with it. Once an adult has decided to leave, it should be worked on with the other adults and then with the children. A therapeutic principle is that the time needed to work on an ending should reflect the time in the therapeutic situation. The longer an adult has been working with a child, the more notice the child will need. Three or four months would be a minimum length of time for children to know about the leaving of a key carer. The timing of the actual leaving is also significant. Some of the feelings associated with leaving emerge after the person has gone, however much anticipation there has been. Ideally, the house should be together for a few weeks after the leaving to understand what everyone feels about it and what, if anything, needs to be done. The middle of session is probably the best time for this.

While providing an uninterrupted one-to-one relationship is a key part of our work, overemphasizing this can lead to a number of potential difficulties. If we perceive a leaving as catastrophic to the work with an individual child, while the leaving may actually be shocking, the child is not without support. Hopefully, he has a team of concerned adults who will continue to care and think about him. He will also have different relationships with these adults. If we overemphasize the uninterrupted one-to-one relationship, whenever it cannot be provided this may provoke excessive guilt and responsibility as if we are letting the children down. This could give the children a message unconsciously that we are not good enough. It is possible we will idealize the one-to-one relationship in a similar way that the mother-infant relationship can be idealized. Though the mother-infant relationship is central to the infant's development, it is not always the primary carer whom the infant has his strongest attachment with. The children we work with are emotionally unintegrated not just because of failings in their parental relationships, but also because of the lack of a significant other – a person who could have helped, as both a support to their parents, or to acknowledge and understand their own distress.

A team's continuity is essential to each child's treatment. If there are any temporary arrangements for a child's care, it is essential that he knows the whole team is thinking about him and his needs. His day-to-day care should be organized in a way that is as clear as possible to him and the team. Even if it is only temporary, there should be a nominated person responsible for overseeing this, to provide regular individual contact with the child and to communicate with parents and social worker.

The transition between carers when a child's carer leaves

A new carer may seem like yet another disruption in the child's life and because of his reaction to this, we may fear he will be unable to accept care from that person. This raises questions about how the child's needs can be met during this change.

When it is clear that a focal-carer is leaving, should her role be taken over by someone else before she leaves? The specific nature of the relationship between the child and focal-carer is important. Has it been a long relationship? Is there dependency involved? Is the relationship in the early stages and not established? If the relationship is not particularly established it can be difficult for the adult who is leaving to provide the level of emotional involvement needed to help the child become established in his treatment. If the relationship has been long and established, more attention will need to be paid to the ending. In this case the adult's gradual withdrawal before leaving could be helpful to the child.

An adult's feelings about leaving also need careful consideration. Is the wish to hand over care and treatment connected to a wish to get things over quickly and to avoid some of the difficult feelings involved? The staff team should work on these matters together. If the adult leaving feels concern for the child and his needs, and the team shares this, then the decision made about his care will convey this concern to the child. On the other hand, if there is resentment towards the adult leaving and disagreement about the child's care and treatment, this will also be picked up by him. If we know who the new carer is going to be, it may be tantalizing for the child not to be told. If we know, we should tell him. However, the new carer and the team should give the child the opportunity and space to experience the loss, and for how he feels about it to emerge and be worked with. If we do not know who is going to look after the child, it is best to tell him that the whole team will be thinking about him and what he needs until they know who the best adult to do that is.

If another adult does become the focal-carer before the present one leaves, the two will need to work closely together on potential conflicts and anxieties, as well as on general matters connected to the handover. This may enable the child to have a positive experience of being handed over in a caring and thoughtful way. We should aim to have a period between a child hearing that his focal-carer is leaving and who the next one is going to be. This is to help acknowledge feelings of loss and change. However, the amount of space possible will depend upon the degree of anxiety involved and what is containable. To help give a sense of continuity over time, the house manager will need to be involved in talking the decision through with the child. This reinforces the message to the child that the whole team thinks about him while change is going on.

The introduction of a new child to the house and school

The beginning of a new placement is obviously of crucial significance to a child and the home he is moving into. However, it is easy to not pay enough attention to this and do the necessary work in preparation.

Before a new child's arrival, adults will assess his needs in detail. Children in his house will also have been informed that he is coming and have the opportunity to think about this, express what they feel and ask questions.

Whoever is going to be the child's focal-carer should be there when he arrives to welcome him. The child will need to be introduced to his surroundings gradually, giving him an opportunity to get to know small areas and widening out from there. To do too much at once could be quite overwhelming for him and make it difficult to establish real contact with any one person.

What could happen is that on arrival, a child will spend his first few days in the house, getting to know all of the staff team, his carer, the other children and daily routines. This could also include doing things like shopping, cooking and a tour of the Community. The teachers from his class will arrange a visit to the school with them outside of school hours. This will allow the child to explore the area and to meet with his teachers without distraction. It will also allow him and the teachers to get to know each other. Having made this initial connection it will be more possible for the child to feel that the teachers are concerned for him when he is with the group. Having done this, his time in the school will be built up gradually to include both the experience of going to school with the group and joining individually at other times.

Change of leadership and possible impact

The leaving of the organization's leader is a major event in the life of the organization. Inevitably, it will have an impact on the staff, the children and the dynamics of the organization. When this happened at the Community it was difficult.

After a long time working in the Community and in the role of principal, the knowledge of his leaving seemed quick, abrupt and to some extent shocking. The change related to the principal's leaving is very significant in itself. There are likely to be many knock-on effects, some of which will not be realized until the principal has actually gone. The way in which things unfold and develop will partly depend upon the way we work with this change. As well as having anxieties there will also be possibilities of growth. A time like this could encourage a review of practice, for example, there may be things we have been doing which we realize we do not need to continue, or things that could be done differently or better.

An effective task-orientated leader inevitably represents a degree of safety and stability. Partly, this is the reality of effective leadership through containment and partly an illusory quality invested in the leader. A change of leadership might therefore threaten our sense of safety. This could lead to increased difficulties in our work with children and our ability to contain them safely.

For some the principal and the Community were so strongly associated with each other that his leaving almost felt like a physical part of the Community leaving. The loss of the leader is potentially intertwined with a greater sense of loss. It may seem as if whatever is invested in the leader will also be lost. To some extent, the principal represented the history of the Community and in particular the psychodynamic tradition. The principal may also represent the symbolic protector of the Community's work. There could be an anxiety that the therapeutic approach will not survive and that the Community's identity will be lost.

At this time, we may feel anxious that our preoccupation might not be sufficient or 'good enough' to emotionally hold the children. If we feel temporarily anxious about our capacity to work safely, then reducing the number of difficult children could be an unconscious defensive reaction to the principal's leaving. It may seem like this will release some of our resources to help us survive this change. In the short term there could be some relief but in the long term children are only likely to feel contained and secure when they sense we can hold onto them and work through whatever difficulties we are faced with.

Following the initial period of loss, work is needed to take back what has been projected onto the leader. While there may be anxiety related to loss and survival, it is important we recognize the capacities we actually have within us. The therapeutic culture has been internalized within staff members and the Community's structures. Maintaining this belief can be difficult, partly because we are likely to feel more vulnerable during a time of major change and because the nature of our work is closely connected to feelings of self-doubt.

Endings produce different reactions. To preserve and protect the image of the person leaving, it is possible that we try to avoid difficulties that might rock the boat. Ending the placements of some of our most difficult children could be seen in this context. It could also be seen in a different way, as spoiling the ending by attacking the work – the principal leaves a depleted rather than a thriving Community. Leavings are likely to stir up some angry feelings related to a sense of being abandoned and rejected. The relatively sudden nature of the leaving may have added to this and there could be disappointment about the nature of the ending.

At this time, the Community had been dealing with a lot of change, much of which felt imposed externally rather than as an outcome of an internal process. This can feel like something is being taken away or stolen.

Chapter 13

External Reality and Protection from Impingement (intolerable disruption and stimulation)

Prolonged impingement on the self is traumatic. During infancy a mother will protect the infant from impingement (excessive stimuli), so that the infant experiences a sense of continuing self without intolerable disruption. Infants need protection from excesses of emotional and physical stimulation. Infants who do not have adequate protection will develop reactions to impingement.

> Reacting at this stage of human development means a temporary loss of identity. This gives an extreme sense of insecurity and lays the basis for an expectation of further examples of loss of continuity of self, and even a congenital (but not inherited) hopelessness in respect of the attainment of a personal life. (Winnicott, 1949, p.183)

In work with traumatized children, we will need to provide protection from impingement. This will allow the child to feel safe and provide him with this essential developmental experience. The level of protection the child needs is likely to be that of a younger child.

Children using toys and magazines with violent and offensive images

The toys and magazines available to young people have become increasingly graphic with exciting and provocative images. Young people will be drawn towards this and there could be some value in this in terms of their development and identity as a person separate to their parents. However, the question as to whether these images are helpful to the child or potentially confusing and overwhelming needs to be looked at. Particularly in work with traumatized children, adults must manage the environment to protect the child from unhelpful stimulation.

There are a variety of toys, computer games and magazines with particularly violent and gruesome images portrayed in graphic detail. Such images come with an already imposed fantasy world. In ordinary childhood, the parental role would be to protect the emotionally unintegrated child from such powerful external stimulation that leaves him feeling overwhelmed, invaded and impotent. As the children we work with have experienced severe deprivation of parental protection, it is essential that we provide this role for them as part of the therapeutic environment.

These toys and magazines referred to are not appropriate for unintegrated children to have at the Community. Parents, foster parents and social workers should be asked for their support. Whatever the children experience outside of the Community (during breaks, for instance), we need to provide them with this barrier and control of what comes back with them.

If an emotionally unintegrated child has such toys and magazines, he should not be asked to keep them to himself in his own room, as a way of managing the situation. This is not providing him with an appropriate level of protection and could be worrying for other children in the group. It may also encourage a false-self type of response in the child. For example, he might agree to manage the situation in a pseudomature way that is not helpful to him. The degree of protection from external stimulation that is appropriate for both individuals and the group needs careful assessment.

The same principles apply to other activities such as television and particularly stimulating games, such as war games, or touching games with each other. Adults should always be involved to ensure the child or children do not lose a sense of being protected from inappropriate stimulation.

How do we manage things children bring back to the house?

While adults working with traumatized children decide upon the kind of toys and materials that are around in the house, children will inevitably find things or acquire things from elsewhere. It can be difficult to know how to respond to a child who has found or bought something that is not appropriate.

In all houses, we have a clear idea of what we allow in the house – toys, books, magazines, videos and all manner of other things ranging from pets to open fires. The underlying idea is that ordinary child development requires the provision of an environment that protects the child from undue, external stimulation. If the child is not protected in this way, he is faced with situations that may make him anxious without having the internal resources to manage them. Winnicott (1964) has described the idea of introducing an infant to the external world in small doses. As the children we work with have been deprived in this area, we provide this protective environment offering the opportunity for this essential experience. Children who have been deprived in this way may not easily accept this type of provision nor believe it can survive. In their experience, periods of feeling appropriately protected have broken down and then failed. They might object to the provision, rubbish it, attack it, undermine it and generally test it. Though this may seem negative, it could be a way of ensuring the environment is protective and of finding out more about it.

How do we respond when children might try to bring things into a house that we feel are not suitable? How do we respond to this situation when it arises? Most importantly, we should try to think what the child is bringing our attention to – what is the communication involved? We can explore this with him. If it is something he is not allowed to have in the house, we should explain this to him. If it is something he is allowed to have at home but not here, we could discuss it with his parents with the view possibly to giving it to them to keep at home. The link between home and here could be an underlying communication from the child, bringing our attention to this. For example, he may bring something from home as a way of letting us know about his home environment.

If the child has been allowed to buy something inappropriate because of a misunderstanding by one of the staff, we could offer to give the child his money back or return the item to the shop. There might be times when a child deliberately buys what he knows he should not have, for example, alcohol or pornography, in which case it may be appropriate for him to face the consequence of having the item taken from him and disposed of.

Working with news items with children

In a parental role, we may feel responsible for discussing contemporary matters with children and ensuring they are informed of the news. However, in work with severely traumatized children, making sense of complex external events can be very difficult and they might have little capacity to manage this.

Emotionally unintegrated children especially are not always ready emotionally to be faced with difficult news stories. Also, there is an issue as to what is news, from whose point of view and from which culture? Unintegrated children do not have the internal resources to make sense of much of what is reported by the media. However, through TV, radio and newspapers, children will pick up news reports. Adults need to be attuned to this and try to help make sense of what it means to the child involved. It can be more helpful to respond to a child's feelings about the issue than to give an informed response to the news item. Matters that are picked up by children can be referred to in group meetings or individually.

It can help introduce children to thinking about external events by passing on news about everyday things such as changes in the seasons, cultural and religious festivals, and other matters that help us in the early years to know about the world.

The massacre at Dunblane (1996)

Staff were strongly affected by the Dunblane school massacre (16 children and teachers were massacred by a gunman) and found a gulf between the meaning it had for them and for the children with whom they were working. Finding a way of bridging this gulf was particularly challenging and demanding. This typifies the difficulty for staff in working on concerns where their own strong feelings contrast so powerfully with the child's apparent attitude.

It is difficult for adults to talk openly about such a tragic and distressing event as Dunblane. The children we work with will not necessarily censure their more primitive emotions and can appear to be unconcerned about the feelings of others. For example, one child pretended to shoot 16 people in his house in a jokey sort of way. We need to be careful how we respond to this kind of behavior and not off-load our feelings in a reactive way onto the children.

Some children have expressed a sense of pathological guilt as if they are somehow responsible for the massacre, possibly connected to a sense of feeling responsible for upsetting their own parents, who they fear may feel like killing them in return. An event such as this may tap into our own violent feelings towards the children and this may disturb us. The sense of a safe place being so violently invaded might have an impact on how safe people feel in other similar settings.

The impact of external processes on treatment

The work we do with traumatized children takes place within an environment created specifically to focus on meeting their needs. However, this is within the context of a wider environment over which we have less control. In particular, looking after children is highly regulated work involving regular intervention and imposition of requirements. Changes imposed by the external environment will impact on our work and can seem to conflict with it. When the impact is significant, we may feel that our task with the children is in jeopardy. This anxiety can be picked up by the children and contribute to the sense that we are failing in meeting their needs. This discussion took place during a major period of external change.

During a period of a few months the Community underwent some major changes, many of which were led by external influences, for example, being taken over by NCH, becoming a school, and dealing with matters raised by investigations and inspections. When this goes on for a long time it can feel as if we are losing a sense of our therapeutic task. How can we work with change in a way that is most conducive to our task?

Some changes in themselves are relatively small, such as being required to use window restrictors on all downstairs bedroom windows. The use of wakeful night staff initially seemed like a major change but has now been incorporated into our approach. Quite often the reaction to the change is mainly influenced by the way it is introduced and the ownership of it. If changes are introduced externally without staff and children's involvement, resistance and resentment are more likely. This can feel as if change is being imposed in an impersonal way.

The accumulative effect of change can also have a wider impact on a culture. For example, if there is a continual emphasis on managing behavior safely, mainly by using physical means, there could be a shift away from attentiveness to other aspects of the work – for instance, the importance of relationships, emotional holding and understanding behavior. If we introduce something like window restrictors, this may be perceived in different ways. A child may feel that we have recognized his need for physical containment, in the same way a parent ensures an infant's environment is safe. It is recognized that the infant will have impulses, reactions and wishes that he is not able to manage safely. Without the safety of this physical management, the infant will not feel emotionally held as a basic need has not been recognized. Emotionally unintegrated children will need to feel physically safe in this way, before they can accept emotionally that they are safe and can become less reliant on external controls.

If the child's behavior is more related to underlying feelings and we only manage the surface behavior, the feelings will still be there and need working with. If we are able to contain a child physically, we might get closer to his feelings and encourage him to communicate. However, if we do not remain attentive, the child may just find another way of driving feelings away, becoming, for example, extremely shut off.

In our parental roles, it can be difficult if other professionals tell us we need to change or improve something. By implication, we could feel it is being suggested that we are not good or caring enough. In effect, all children in care are treated as if they are on an at risk register. The staff caring for the children are constantly checked and monitored, to ensure the children are being looked after properly. While this is part of a collaborative, professional piece of work, which we share with social workers and inspectors among others, those directly involved with the children inevitably feel personally responsible for 'their' children. This will to some extent be true for all professionals involved, but our work with children is particularly about developing strong attachments, and provision normally associated with parent-child relationships. It is also likely, at times, that feelings of being a better parent than the children's birth parents will be evoked. If we are caught up in this feeling, suggestions that we are not good enough will challenge this illusion and be met defensively.

The seemingly contradictory feelings of omnipotence and helplessness are prevalent in the children we work with. The feeling that we should be able to manage everything can act as a defense against feelings of helplessness and despair. It may be difficult in these circumstances to acknowledge our limitations and act upon them – for example, to admit that things are not safe and to take appropriate action. We can be most positive by thinking about our responses to these situations and try to be objective about recommendations and requirements to change our practice.

Chapter 14

Working with Violence and Aggression

Traumatized and deprived children have often experienced extreme violence and may display violence and aggression towards others as well as themselves. Our work in this area is central to the therapeutic process.

Understanding violence and aggression

How do we work with and understand situations that are becoming generally violent and aggressive? To begin work with children who have suffered violence and who might behave violently it is important for them to know that it is not acceptable to be hit and to ensure that they are aware of this.

If we are clear about this, how do we understand violence? Dockar-Drysdale (1990i) claimed that violent acting out is linked to a breakdown in communication:

> One could start by saying that the management of violence is its prevention. By this statement, I mean that, since all acting out is a breakdown in communication, it is our responsibility to keep in communication with the children in our care. (p.127)

Violent behavior can be the expression of feelings that have felt inexpressible in other ways. If violent feelings are not expressed and acknowledged, physical attack may be a primitive way of trying to get through to someone. For these feelings to be communicated there needs to be someone who is receptive to them. Actually hearing or being receptive to violent feelings is not easy. The child could express them indirectly or in a complicated way and the adult might respond defensively. It is possible to see how violence can escalate in this situation. A violent environment makes it more difficult for feelings to be thought about and understood. If the violence or anger can be acknowledged and recognized, it could lead on to discovering other feelings which underlie this, for example, anger can initially feel safer to express than fear or sadness.

We should not automatically be critical of a child for shouting or using abusive language to express himself. It could be difficult for him to find any other way. Violent words are preferable to violent actions and can be a step forwards. Violent and aggressive behavior can be a sign of hope. Trauma in early infancy has the effect of numbing an infant's senses, in a way that can feel annihilating. Aggressive behavior may give the child a sense of being alive or coming to life and strong feelings evoked in others might also create this sense. Sexualized behavior can have a similar effect.

Due to the severity of a child's deprivation he may actually need to experience physical holding. If a child is in a panic-rage or behaving dangerously he may need, whatever the reason for it, to be held safely and firmly. There are occasions when an emotionally unintegrated child experiences rage similar to a toddler's tantrum. This could be regarded as part of 'normal' development related to feelings of frustration and being overwhelmed. Dockar-Drysdale (1971) argues:

> The 'ordinary devoted mother' (Winnicott) can contain the baby's rage and her own feelings as long as this is necessary – until the baby can contain his own feelings. Many of the children in our care have not become containers: at five, ten or fifteen years they may still need a lot of containment in order to integrate into whole, containing people. In the meantime, they are liable to act out their intolerably violent emotions in many ways, damaging to other people, themselves and their environment. Winnicott defined panic as 'unthinkable anxiety'. Much violence is caused by panic states: *thinking* is an essential way of containing feelings. (p.123)

Where our attempts to think about the child and communicate with him fail to prevent his feelings escalating into violence, we may need to physically intervene to ensure safety. This intervention may vary in scale from holding his hand to physical restraint. Inevitably, we can become anxious about physical restraint. We will have our own anxieties about restraining children, as well as those related to external concerns, such as having allegations made against one. Some of this anxiety and doubt may create a sense of suspicion that we cannot be trusted with these children. This anxiety could diminish our capacity to manage children safely. Whatever the reality of the external matters, we need to question how we use them. For instance, do they evoke in us, at times, a feeling of wanting to hurt or punish the children? Whether this is in fantasy or reality, guilt will be attached to this. The 'threat' of having allegations made against one could bring to the surface these feelings of guilt and a fear of being discovered.

Staff should discuss and try to understand the feelings evoked in them through their involvement with the children. For example, it is usual for staff in team meetings to discuss aggressive or punitive feelings. It can be more difficult to acknowledge and communicate about sexual matters in a general sense and specifically in connection with physical restraint. It is essential that we try to acknowledge and be conscious of these underlying anxieties.

How do we respond to particularly violent attacks on staff by children?

A sudden violent attack by a child or young person on a staff member makes it difficult to work out how to respond appropriately. There could be immediate difficulties in managing the practicalities of the situation, as well as the strong feelings involved. Without prior thought and guidelines about these situations, it is easy for our responses to become overreactive and uncontained. Should we have guidelines to ensure a consistent response?

There is no formal internal complaints procedure for staff regarding a child's behavior, however violent it is. When working with the complaints procedure for children, it can be difficult to reconcile, for example, receiving allegations that may be unfounded while at the same time having no similar option to complain if violently hurt by a child.

When a staff member is attacked, the following approaches offer different ways of responding:

- The staff member who has been attacked might work with the child directly, saying what she thought about the attack and giving the child a firm message about his behavior. The focus may be on trying to help the child get in touch with any sense of concern he has. This can lead to reparation from the child. The team can work together in supporting this work.
- The house manager might intervene more directly, sometimes having the child removed from the group or even the house. The emphasis here is on giving the child a clear message about the seriousness of his behavior. Gradually and in a planned way, further work can go on as described above.

- A further stage in this process is to involve the child's social worker and sometimes parents in acknowledging and working with what has happened.
- A more senior manager than the staff member may also be involved by giving the child a clear message about his behavior and by working with his social worker.
- None of the above suggestions exclude involving the police. This could help the child face the reality of what he has done, while also again stressing the seriousness of the attack.

Obviously, there are many different therapeutic and management concerns involved in each situation. The exact nature of the incident will need to be explored carefully. Assessment of the child and serious discussion within the staff team can all help to develop a better understanding of the incident, the child's needs, and the appropriate management and therapeutic approach.

Following a violent attack, the staff member will need support. The opportunity to talk about the incident, feelings connected to it and possible responses should be offered as soon as possible. This can be with someone in the team or with someone outside the team. The closer to the incident, the more helpful this is likely to be. The staff member's feelings and anxiety levels might be affected for a number of days or weeks after the incident. The incident may need to be talked through a number of times, exploring the nature of the incident in detail once it is possible to feel less emotional about it.

Consider the complexity of all this – for instance, does a child's stage of emotional development make a difference to our response? How do we work with the child's own history of violence and abuse? How much responsibility is the child's and how much the staff member's? The child might be distressed or frightened by the incident. He could be too afraid to show this and appear unconcerned. He may actually be unable to feel concern. How do the team support the person attacked, provide individual attention for the child and create a sense of safety for the group of children? If attention is given to the child and his needs, this might feel disloyal to the person he has attacked. There may be a wish to punish the child and not provide him with any support and understanding.

How do we take violence seriously?

While understanding that we will need to work with violence in some form or other, this acceptance can also seem like we are condoning the violence. This question of how we take violence seriously is often asked in our work and particularly following episodes of violent behavior from children. It can have different meanings at different times. For instance, the question may imply that the person who has been attacked or another staff member should do something to show they are taking it seriously. It may be felt that the child should be punished to match the level of his violent behavior. There could be an underlying anxiety that staff are identified with the violence and are colluding with it by not doing enough about it.

Children need to understand that staff do not expect to be hit, that it hurts and it is not the way to treat someone. This can be difficult to understand or believe for children who have not experienced the type of care which we seek to offer and who may expect all relationships to be violent. A child also understands what we intend by the way we care for him and each other. Hopefully, during time his experience of this will be internalized by him. The child can understand, too, that violence is taken seriously if we worry and think about it with him and each other.

For a child to get a sense that his violence can be survived, we need to be able to care for him safely. It is also important to be open to his capacity for reparation. We need to understand the limits and potential each child has in terms of reparation. If a child hurts us, we can show him the consequences of his actions and the impact on oneself as a feeling person. There are dangers that we become numbed by violence if it is experienced regularly. There will be times when an individual or team is less able to give the message that it is not okay to be hurt. We should be attentive and supportive towards each other.

A child's intention to hurt, even if he is stopped, needs tackling in a similar way. If we take violence seriously, we still cannot expect a specific response from a child. He may or may not show or be able to show concern. However, we can assess the nature of the violence and his response to it by how safe we feel it is to work with him. At times, it can feel that there is a disparity between our approach and the reality of the children's behavior. We might feel that we are trying to work with behavior that would not be tolerated in the outside world. This conflict can occur particularly in relation to the law. If the police are involved, is this unhelpful or does it bring in a necessary reality? Also, we will have our own internal dilemmas, related to our own experiences, especially during childhood. Feelings of injustice, of wanting to punish, seek revenge or teach a lesson are often brought to the surface.

How do we understand a child who harms, injures or kills a living creature?

The act of killing small creatures, such as insects, is common in childhood. However, there is a point where this can raise concern. Traumatized children may reenact their own experiences by harming and killing creatures. If we are not attentive and responsive to this behavior, it is more likely to develop rather than be worked through.

We could all think of examples where a child had injured or killed an insect. Often in childhood, there is a sadistic fascination with these creatures. Many of us can recall killing, dissecting or maiming insects, pulling legs and wings off. In one of our houses a group of children had been catching flies, some wanted to kill them and others to look after them.

There can be a distinction between insects and other small animals such as mice or rabbits. If a child has some idea a creature does not have feelings like a person, then he may think that it is acceptable to kill or maim it. An emotionally unintegrated child has little capacity to recognize his own feelings or those of others. He has not reached a stage where he can feel much concern for others or feel guilt in relation to his actions. He may also have aggressive feelings or impulses that he is unable to manage or contain without the support of a grown-up. An unintegrated child cannot clearly distinguish between life and death. For example, a child pointed to a sheep running about and asked if it was the one that had died recently. A child at this stage who does kill something might also believe that he can bring it back to life. An example of this was another child who breathed on dead flies trying to do just that.

In early development, an infant may sense any frustration or pain he feels as an attack from a hostile world. Living creatures could actually seem quite frightening and fierce to him. Or he might desire the animal but discover that the animal acts differently than he expects, for example, by being aggressive or rejecting towards him. This may challenge the child's omnipotence and he may feel persecuted. A child who is just beginning to be aware of his dependence and vulnerability might hurt or kill a small creature as a way of feeling powerful and in control. A child may project his own fears onto a creature, which then represents those feelings for the child. The child can then get rid of his fear by getting rid of the creature. Similarly, if a child feels vulnerable and dependant but is unable to contain those feelings, he might project them onto an animal and attack the animal representing those parts of him.

At the stage where a child is beginning to feel concern, he will find it difficult to contain aggressive feelings towards a grown-up he also cares about. He could feel anxious about hurting the grown-up and act out his feelings towards other things, people or creatures. A child who has been abused and in the role of a victim might act this out with small creatures. This could involve cruelty where the child makes the animal suffer in a way he has been made to suffer. The cornered animal may represent how the child has been made to feel. If a child's hurting or killing of an animal is secretive, this might suggest that he has an idea it is wrong or bad. Another distinction can be made if the child's behavior towards the animal is sustained and planned rather than impulsive. An unintegrated child does not usually have the capacity to think about things in a sequence.

All of this relates to a child and his own development. It is necessary to question how the dynamics of a child's environment have an impact upon his feelings and behavior. For example, if a child's parents feel like hurting each other but are unable to acknowledge it, the child may become a receptacle for their feelings. He might be unable to contain these feelings and draw attention to them by actually hurting something himself. His own aggressive feelings could be amplified by his parents' unacknowledged aggression. The same dynamics can arise in our own work.

We have to consider the possibilities that arise here. When individual cases are being examined, it can help to start with a range of possibilities. This will help us to decide the most appropriate way of approaching the particular situation.

Physical restraint – what we learn from training

Staff had been training in working with challenging behavior and physical restraint. This particular training recommended that staff do not talk with a child during the actual restraint. This was a new approach within the Community and different to Dockar-Drysdale's (1990g) view that it is important to talk to the child in a calm way about what is happening.

The reason for this recommendation is to reduce stimuli to a minimum until the child has calmed. A child who needs to be restrained is in a highly charged state and it is likely the grown-ups involved are strongly affected. The emotional content of the situation is powerful and this, along with the physical exertion that is required, contributes to physiological changes such as high adrenaline levels. This makes it difficult for the grown-up to talk with the child in a way that actually helps to calm rather than fuel the situation. Sometimes things said by grown-ups involved with a child who is in a panic-rage are unhelpful and can be quite angry. This highlights the point that it is better for two grown-ups to be involved, providing support for each other as well as for the child. It often works better if the person holding the child is not the one who has just been attacked by the child.

Contrary to this approach, Dockar-Drysdale (1990g) recommended that grown-ups talk with a child during a panic about the panic.

> It is essential to talk to him in a quiet voice throughout the whole experience, emphasizing that he will soon be better, that the worker understands that the boy cannot help what he is doing – that he is in a state of anxiety beyond fear and that one day he will not have to panic any more, as we come to understand him. (p.123)

She also believed that children could hear what was being said and often remembered it later, even if it did not seem like they could hear anything at the time. If such an approach can be achieved in practice, the child may experience it as caring and containing. The grown-up is providing some meaning to the situation and might be felt by the child to be more present than if she were completely silent. The tone of voice is as significant as what is being said. Even if the child cannot hear all of the words, he may be able to perceive a tone that sounds comforting and nonthreatening. This is similar to the kind of words and sounds a parent makes while holding a baby that is distressed. The grown-up is speaking to the frightened child and not to the anger or rage. At these times everything that is said should be to do with holding the panic and not questioning the child about what has happened or being critical of him. The words used should name what is happening in a way that is clear and understandable. If a child is in a panic, the panic can be named in some way. For example, with some children it has helped to say 'we are holding the upset'. The word 'panic' itself could be used, as it is specific but it is also an everyday word that most people can relate to. We could explain to a child and his parents that when he panics it is like the feeling that most of us experience on occasions, but instead of lasting a short while goes on and on until it is unbearable. Words used during the actual restraint should be familiar to the child. If it is difficult to talk in a way that is clearly helpful to him, it might be better to say nothing until he is feeling calmer.

At all times, concentration on the child's physical safety is the priority and nothing should distract from this. If the grown-ups are not talking to the child but are able to hold him securely and safely, the child will gradually feel the physical security that is being asserted safely and caringly. The principle of not talking is positive in the sense that we should only say something if we are clear that it is actually helpful. A degree of silence can also enable the grown-up to pay more attention to what she is doing. We should remind ourselves of the power of the grown-up who is holding a child, especially to be aware of punitive and retaliatory feelings that can be evoked in these situations.

Following the restraint, an opportunity for the child and grown-up to talk about the experience is essential. The timing of this will be most helpful where those involved are sufficiently recovered to be able to think and talk about the experience but close enough to the actual incident so that it still feels real to them. It can be helpful for the child and grown-up to talk together, maybe with a third person. The child and grown-up will also need some individual work and support. The aim of this work is to give those who restrained the child a chance to discuss what happened, to describe how they felt, to reflect and see if anything can be learnt or recognized from the experience. This may help to find different ways of working with the difficulty that built up to the panic and caused the restraint. Obviously, the emphasis between the child and grown-up in this work will largely be related to the child's level of emotional integration. The less integrated the child, the more responsibility the grown-ups will take for the situation. Emotionally unintegrated children can begin by naming feelings and making small connections, but even the naming of feelings may take a long time and will need a lot of support from a grown-up.

Now that we are using specific restraint techniques, we could show and explain the methods we use to children, parents and social workers; then everyone would be clear about why and how physical restraint is used. Clarity and support may help to contain everyone's anxieties. Clearly, some children will only be able to make limited sense of this and will need to test and find things out for themselves.

Gender issues in relation to the therapeutic management of violence and physical restraint

Historically, it was normally the role of male carers to manage children if physical restraint was necessary. At the same time, female carers were predominantly involved in nurturing roles. These roles have become increasingly shared between female and male carers. However, there will be gender issues involved and we should consider what these are for us and each child.

By definition, work with emotionally unintegrated children will include acting out. A child who has suffered deprivation and abuse before emotional integration has taken place will not be able to differentiate between his experiences and feelings. The experiences cannot be internalized and known about by him and so are acted out. The first stages in treatment are for the grown-ups safely to contain this acting out and to think about it with each other. Gradually the experience of being thought about in this way enables the child to begin thinking about his own experiences and to integrate them.

Initially, as the child carries an indigestible sense of trauma, it is likely he may feel that the grown-ups attempting to work with him are abusive.

Throughout the history of the Community's work, there have been occasions of violent acting out by children but its extent fluctuates. Physical restraint and women's involvement in this have raised questions in relation to the therapeutic task. The reason for this is linked to the role of women as maternal figures and the anxieties involved for children in being restrained by a maternal figure, with a risk of injuring that person. Traumatized children often have powerful fantasies of destroying and being destroyed by a maternal figure. Children should be protected from the fear that this acute anxiety could turn into reality. Though men are maternal figures for some children, this is normally within the context of a specific relationship such as focal-carer, rather than to a group of children as a whole. It is felt that the actual gender difference means women are more likely than men to embody a maternal role. In recent years, more emphasis has been placed on the nature of the actual relationship between a grown-up and child rather than the gender differences.

If staff were not involved in physical restraint based on gender, what kind of feelings could this evoke? How might it affect the way men and women are perceived by children and each other? Do we need to provide children with a sense of difference between men and women in this area? To what extent do boys actually need men and girls need women to identify with? Boys and girls are aggressive in different ways. Some of this is innate and some of it socially influenced. Because of their own experiences, do men and women understand and respond to children's aggression differently?

Physical restraint and physical holding

Physical restraint means the minimum use of physical force needed to safely prevent harm or injury. A child in a panic who is being violent and out of control will probably need what feels like restraint but this is a part of his treatment and can be therapeutic if worked with effectively (see Dockar-Drysdale 1990g, 1990h, 1990i). A child in a panic may need restraining safely before he can be reached emotionally. Sometimes a child is in a flight from panic and will not actually panic until stopped. The flight from the panic, which often involves manic behavior, can be more unsafe than being physically stopped.

We may feel that we are physically holding rather than restraining when we are more in touch with a child emotionally. This might be following a violent rage or preempting a panic-rage by successful early anticipation. Anxiety about physical holding and restraint, partly related to the legal aspect, can inhibit our work. Grown-ups might feel vulnerable if they discuss it openly. Other feelings can also inhibit us in this area, for example, feelings of guilt and responsibility in relation to the children's difficulties or any aggressive feelings we have towards their behavior. Difficulties are most likely to arise when these feelings are not acknowledged.

Bullying

It is relatively recent, since the Children Act 1989, that children's homes have been required to have a policy on bullying. The term 'bully' is now clearly defined and used frequently, though it can tend to be used in a very general way to describe a multitude of situations.

It is important to be clear what we think is bullying behavior and what is the intention behind the act. At what point do we think behavior bullying or a child capable of bullying? Frequency is often used to distinguish bullying. Bullying is persistent rather than a one-off incident such as a fight. All bullying is significant and there will be procedures to follow to ensure an appropriate and consistent response. Procedures do not deal with the problem unless there is continual exploration and thinking to accompany them. It is essential in our work that we should always try to understand behavior and what it means to individuals and groups. A policy that emphasizes the importance of understanding is less likely to run the risk of perpetuating bullying.

Working with severely deprived children means that power and the relationship of abuser and abused, bully and victim are central to what we do. Powerful feelings are evoked with dynamics, which can pull everyone into different roles. This may be, for example, the roles of bully, victim and rescuer. It is essential to be ever-conscious of these dynamics and our own role.

All the children we work with are victims. Our work is to try to enable children to be in a position where they can make a choice to be neither a bully nor a victim. This will involve working with any aspect of a child that seems destructive to him or others. As well as working with issues as they arise, the whole aim of our therapeutic approach is to facilitate emotional development and the capacity for concern. Children who feel concern for others are not likely to bully.

Chapter 15

Working with Strong Feelings and Supervision

Work with traumatized children can evoke strong and primitive feelings. Supervision offers the opportunity where they can be discussed, thought about and understood. The supervisor provides a form of emotional containment, which helps the person supervised make sense of her work. This work can be confusing, chaotic, incomprehensible and overwhelming. The supervisor provides emotional holding. This process also provides a model of how the staff member can help the child.

The supervisor's task

The therapeutic resource in each team had the responsibility for providing supervision to individual staff on their therapeutic work. This type of supervision was distinct to that provided by the team manager and helped to ensure that the chance to think about the work with children remained central and was not adversely dominated by management concerns. While this discussion is primarily about the supervision of therapeutic work, there are aspects of it that also apply to other forms of supervision.

Supervision is about:

- Ensuring that each team member is aware of therapeutic matters and understands the basic approach. Within this, a check is kept of an individual child's treatment, ensuring that each child's needs are being thought about and responded to.

- Providing a space where the supervised person can bring any concerns and feelings to explore them. The supervisor's role here is to be attentive, thinking about all aspects of what is being presented. The opportunity for the person who is being supervised to talk through something and be listened to, will enable her to make more sense of the matter or to see it differently. The supervisor might also have useful observations, thoughts or advice about the situation.
- Training – the supervisor may think it appropriate to work on a theoretical aspect of the work, linking theory to practice.
- Managing in the sense of giving direction where necessary. There are many areas of our treatment task where we have clear policy and guidelines. This is always linked to good practice, whether it is basic child care or therapeutic work.
- Providing a reliable and protected space for the supervision. Supervision should have a reliable time and place, and be as free as possible from interruption.

These different elements of supervision are not always easy to balance. For instance, the supervisor could feel there is a conflict between letting the person being supervised lead the meeting and taking the lead with an issue, listening and teaching, talking and not talking, and the many different matters the time could be used for. There are no easy solutions to these dilemmas. The dilemmas in themselves, if we think about them, may give some understanding of what is going on in the supervision and in the work outside of it.

The supervisor should think about her feelings during, before and after the supervision, as these could be directly connected to the work with the person whom she is supervising. What the staff member brings to the supervision will not just be in the form of words, but also in nonverbal and unconscious communication. Often the feelings evoked in the supervision setting will be a reflection of what is going on outside of it. For example, a staff member who is working with a depressed child but is not in touch with those feelings might unconsciously evoke them in the supervisor.

Finally, the supervisor needs to think about the feelings that she brings to the supervision in relation to the supervision and other matters If these are not conscious, they could be played out in the supervision. For example, a supervisor can consciously or unconsciously encourage a staff member to behave in a certain way by conveying messages such as: 'Don't talk to me about problems, I have enough on my plate' or 'Please have some difficulties, I'm feeling a bit useless and need someone I can help.'

The model of supervision described is appropriate to the therapeutic task and the issues involved closely reflect the kind of struggles we have in our work with children.

Supervision with a staff member who has been physically attacked by a child

Supervision during this time can have a major impact on the adult who has been attacked and the work taking place with the child. As well as this situation being difficult for the adult who has been attacked, it can also evoke strong feelings in the supervisor, who needs to think about her own feelings in relation to the incident.

The person attacked might have strong feelings about the incident which can sometimes continue for long periods. Where the incident has led to a temporary impasse between the adult and child, the supervisor could feel torn between the difficulty the adult is experiencing and the child's need for care and provision from that adult. The supervisor is thinking about the child's treatment and the adult who has suffered violence.

In supervision it is important to support the adult and to try to empathize with the suffering she is experiencing. However, violent incidents often happen for a combination of complex reasons and we should be careful how we react to the child and apportion blame for the incident. The child may have some responsibility that he needs help to think about. If he does not have the emotional capacity to make reparation, he will not be able to understand his destructiveness. Only when he feels that he can repair as well as damage, will he be able to feel any real concern for himself and others.

A child needs to understand that it is unacceptable to hurt people. If this is done in a nonblaming way it is less likely he will feel overwhelmingly confused. If he has previously experienced violence from those closest to him, it will not be easy for him to make sense of our responses. We might feel a pressure to blame or punish the child and to not do this can feel as if we are colluding with his behavior.

When an attacked staff member says that she no longer wants to care for the child or to be with him, it is important to maintain the faith that the adult will in time become empathetic. She may need the supervisor temporarily to hold onto these feelings, partly as a way of protecting the child from them. If the supervisor begins work too soon with the adult on understanding the child and his needs, the adult may feel a lack of concern for her. If the adult who has been attacked is reassured of the opportunity for reflection and concern, it is more likely that she will be able to think about the wider matters. Once that stage has been reached, it will be productive to explore the whole situation in greater depth.

Staff working in a child-centered way with children can tend to neglect their own needs at times. Following a violent incident a staff member might sometimes need help to stop and attend to her own needs. On the other hand, the adult could find herself shocked by her negative feelings towards the child. Given our conscious motivations in doing this work, discovering uncaring, unforgiving, revengeful or hateful aspects of ourselves can be disturbing. If these feelings can be thought about rather than reacted to defensively, there is potential for growth in these difficult situations.

Work with children towards whom we have powerful angry feelings

Emotional involvement with children can evoke strong feelings. At some point most children will experience the anger of an adult and this can be important in the child's development. However, in work with traumatized and deprived children these feelings can be experienced more intensely and for prolonged periods. This can test our resilience and feel as if we cannot be doing the child or ourselves any good. Finding a way of working with these feelings is crucial to helping a child in the therapeutic process.

At different times, an adult may feel very angry towards a particular child. Sometimes these feelings could be quite hateful and aggressive and might be connected to a specific incident or a more general situation.

As part of normal development, it is necessary for a child to experience limits to what will be tolerated and to discover angry feelings in those caring for him (see Winnicott 1947). If the adult can have these feelings but not express them destructively, this helps give the child a sense that his angry feelings can also be contained. Also, if the child is able to have an impact on another person by, for instance, making her angry, this can help give him a sense that his feelings are real. If he is unable to get through to someone in this way, he could feel threatened and persecuted as if he is of no significance. If an adult feels angry towards a child, it is important not to deny it. The child will pick up these feelings consciously and unconsciously and will be confused if they are denied. There are different ways for the adult to acknowledge these feelings, for example, to herself, to another adult or to the child. The appropriate way will depend upon the particular child and situation.

The adult might be unable to talk much with the child or to carry on daily routines as normal. This could help give a sense of reality to the child. However, the adult might wish to punish or hurt the child and needs to be careful not to express these feelings. When talking with a child we should use language he is most likely to understand, for example, 'I am angry with you because you hurt me.' Although the concept of hate may be understandable from the adult's point of view, the child might easily misunderstand it in a way that is not helpful. Hate can sound like a very powerful feeling that is not related to a specific incident and is long-lasting. Anger may feel more specific and easier to recover from. If we describe our feelings to a child, we should admit that this is what we feel rather than attribute them to him. For example, we could say, 'I am feeling angry with you' rather than 'You are making me feel angry.' This helps to make a distinction or boundary between oneself and the child and lets the child know that he is not in control of our feelings. We can give a child the sense that we are able to be angry while also still holding onto our concern for him. For instance, we can feel angry with a child but at the same time ensure his care is not neglected. If an adult feels unable to be with or do something for him, she can explain this and arrange for someone else to do it. Experiencing this is helpful to children who are unable to hold different feelings together at the same time.

These situations are difficult and need working on carefully between the adult and child, in supervision and often with the whole team.

What is our approach to work with a child who we feel is stuck?

Working with children can feel at times as if we are not making any progress and the child is emotionally stuck. If this continues despite our efforts, our belief can be challenged and we could feel pushed into questioning whether the child is rightly placed with us. On the one hand, this might be the time the child most needs us to stick with him but on the other we may be wasting precious time, using approaches that are not helping the child. How should we work with these situations?

Should we have a clear procedure for assessing a child's development and 'treatability' when we feel he is stuck? We use various tools and forums to help us assess each child. These tools can be used in a focused way when we are concerned about a child. We can also hold case conferences with the professionals involved. Sometimes the process of bringing these groups together can help shed light on things. On occasions, sharing the concern in itself can be supportive and help to move things forward.

What does the problem of being stuck represent and mean to us? When we talk of a child or group being stuck, there is also often a feeling of despair. A sense that whatever we do will not make any difference. It can actually be quite important to feel stuck. Being stuck has a feeling of permanence or being fixed, rather than always being in transit and moving on. A child might be letting us know that he will move on when he is ready rather than when we want him to. This could be a positive development for a child who normally tries to comply with what others wish for him. The child may really feel stuck and hopeless himself and need us to contain those feelings for him. Often a child who has felt stuck for a long time suddenly develops in a way that suggests something positive has been going on during the 'stuckness'.

We should also question how we use the idea that something is stuck. A team member or a team as a whole may all have aspects of their own personality and life that feel stuck. These aspects can feel threatening and could be projected unconsciously. Individuals and groups might be unconsciously selected to carry a sense of 'stuckness'. This is a form of scapegoating. Being stuck can also be connected to feeling that a situation is impossible. For example, if a team as a whole is faced with what feels like an impossible task and the anxieties in this are not fully acknowledged, this problem could be located in one part of the team or child group. This can be a way of organizing the anxiety, which enables the team as a whole to feel less threatened, though the part holding the anxiety might be overwhelmed. If this defensive situation persists, the part holding the problem will be perceived to be responsible for the problem. Attempts to solve the problem will fail unless the underlying dynamics change. Feelings of failure and inadequacy can be reinforced as the cycle continues. If the dynamic becomes entrenched with powerful unconscious investment in it, it will be difficult for the defensive aspects to be given up. It will be difficult to believe that the place where the problem is located is not actually the cause of the problem.

Different parts of the team can represent different things for us at different times. An expectation or mythology can build up that lends different unconscious roles to different parts of the team. During times of change, vulnerability and turmoil there will be a greater tendency for these roles to be taken up. Even though this might not feel productive, the familiarity of the internal dynamics can seem safer than the uncertainty of the external threat.

Vulnerability in residential work with children

Therapeutic work with traumatized and deprived children has to some extent always been perceived as a vocation, requiring great commitment and patience. In recent years, the emotional vulnerability of those involved in this work has been reinforced by the vulnerabilities associated with the risks of allegations and investigations.

Traumatized children can evoke an acute sense of vulnerability in us due to their damaging early experiences. The vulnerability can be felt in a number of different ways. Staff feel vulnerable to attacks from the children, both physical and emotional. They are open to attacks from each other, usually in the criticism of each other's work. They can feel susceptible to reproach from friends or family who feel neglected because of the commitment involved in the work. Finally, they are vulnerable to attack from outside agencies through the complaints and inspection procedures. What may be perceived as an attack may, in fact, be constructive and appropriate criticism. However, work with traumatized children can make staff particularly sensitive due to the intense amount of scrutiny they face and this may make them feel as if they are under attack. There is a heightened sense of vulnerability in a dependency relationship in the sense that one party is reliant on the other. Those attracted to work with traumatized children and care work in general can be motivated to do so by the need to make reparation, and therefore can be more susceptible to feelings such as blame. The need to make reparation can be in relation to actual events where the person *knows* she has actually done something wrong or she *feels* this is the case.

On the other hand, the nature of the work can arouse strong and primitive feelings in all involved, which might lead to mistrust where some people feel they are being attacked. For example, the perceived attacks from other care agencies, parents and social workers might in fact be envy. This could be connected to the relationships we have with children and the primary provision, from which others feel excluded. Staff working with children may also have infantile feelings of envy evoked by the care and provision offered to children.

Chapter 16

Management Structure and the Therapeutic Task

It is possible to have management without therapy, but not therapy without management (Menzies Lyth 1979, 1985). Management includes safety, boundaries and all aspects of the organizational structure. Without these conditions traumatized children will not be able to make use of therapeutic work. Feelings of insecurity, anxiety and mistrust are likely to be overwhelming. In residential and institutional settings the management structure of the whole organization is relevant to the therapeutic task. All aspects of this structure will have an impact on the therapeutic task and potentially be internalized by the children. For example, a management structure that allows for little autonomy and responsibility in the staff is not likely to make this happen for the children. All aspects of the management structure should support the therapeutic task.

Management, treatment and safety

Following the Children Act 1989 there was a significant change of emphasis towards ensuring the safety of children. Child protection procedures became increasingly rigorous. One of the impacts of this was that staff became increasingly preoccupied with safety. Finding a balance between appropriate concern for safety and stifling anxiety is a challenge for all people involved with children.

Safety is an increasing concern and preoccupation in the work. The focus on safety comes up in many different areas, for example, child protection, health and safety matters, and staff-to-child ratios. The concern is appropriate and mostly objective. However, there is a danger that our response to safety becomes increasingly one-dimensional. We might need to take one form of action but not exclude others. For example, if children are becoming inappropriately involved with each other at nighttime, we may focus on how we can stop this from happening. If this situation is putting any child at risk, we are responsible to intervene and manage the risk, for example, by increasing the supervision of children. This could help to make the situation safer. However, we should also try to understand why the situation developed and any underlying meaning that has been communicated. In this example, there are many different possibilities, for instance, anxieties connected to separation and nighttimes; the quality of primary provision and preoccupation; and secretive activity between children at nighttime. If we do not think about these possibilities, the underlying problems will not be picked up and are likely to manifest themselves in a different form.

At two ends of the spectrum we could have a culture with thinking but a lack of any other intervention, and another with reactive short-term action but not enough thinking. Anxiety about safety can be generated by both too much and too little emphasis on it. In the attempt to ensure that things are safe, anxiety might be conveyed giving the message that things are not safe. This can then lead to heightened anxiety, followed by further concern about safety and so on. In work with traumatized children, we can expect an attack on our capacity to think. Children who feel worthless and unlovable are also likely to evoke a harsh response towards them. In this situation, restrictive and impersonal responses are more likely than creative, thoughtful ones.

It can be tempting to look for solutions that do not require us to examine our own involvement. For example, does a child hit out because we have not listened to him and he becomes increasingly forceful in his attempt to get attention? Similarly, we might avoid taking concrete action because we find the reality of what is necessary too threatening, such as the need to take personal authority and say 'no' to a child. We are likely to fluctuate between these extremes and our aim should be to find the best balance for meeting children's needs.

The appropriate approach will be influenced by the overall context within which we work. Much has changed significantly in recent years, both in society as a whole and in social work. Parents have to pay more attention to external factors and influences which affect family life and development. Residential child care workers need to consider myriad factors within their daily work. A small example is the requirement to keep a record of fridge temperatures and food samples. While this is good practice and a necessary part of care provision, the attention required could detract from thinking about other matters.

Each staff role has an increasing focus (to varying degrees) on external matters. The management of the boundary between internal and external reality has always been central to our work. In that sense, things have not changed. The change is mainly one of emphasis. We are now more outward looking than we were. Given these changes, we need to ensure we do not lose our internal focus on treatment. The role of the therapeutic resource is central in keeping this focus and thinking alive for everyone in the team.

The whole environment must be organized and managed in such a way that therapeutic work can be facilitated. There must be a reasonable sense of order for grown-ups to make provision and children to feel secure enough to receive and make use of it. An organizational structure needs to be developed with the aim of establishing a reliable facilitating environment. This structure includes a clear understanding of tasks, roles and responsibility. Boundaries between and within these areas need to be clear. This helps create conditions within which staff can develop appropriate personal and professional authority. Management is more related to the detail of working with children and groups. This includes taking control where necessary to ensure safety and to protect provision so that children's needs are met. The need is to ensure that a balanced focus is kept on everything necessary to create the holding environment within which treatment can take place.

Contact between senior managers and houses

Senior managers had the role of providing 24 hours a day on-call support to the teams working in the houses. This support was by telephone and, if necessary, directly hands-on. The question of how much direct contact senior managers should have with the houses was one of continual review and would become more prominent when a house was experiencing major difficulties. Effective management of the boundary between the house and the wider organization is critical to the work with the children.

Senior managers spending time in houses is often an issue for debate and one about which there can be quite different views and feelings. If senior managers visit houses regularly, they will be more familiar to children and staff whom they see less often outside of the house. If there is discussion in houses about senior managers it may seem as if we are talking about a real person rather than a distant figure. It could also seem as if senior managers know children and staff better by actually seeing and meeting them in houses. This view has to be balanced by the model of working, whereby we feel we can know someone through each other. For example, a supervisor or consultant can know a child through the work she does with the team that works with a child. In work with children who are emotionally fragmented we are familiar with the concept that 'it takes a group to know an individual'. This also raises the issue of individual perception and how the presence of the individual changes the dynamics of the situation. If a senior manager visits a house to see or be shown, to what extent does the visit itself influence what is being seen or shown?

There are occasions when basic care and health and safety matters are checked by senior managers in houses. Even if the atmosphere does change in a house during a senior manager's visit, many other aspects of the house such as the general state of repair and culture can be observed. In addition, things the house is less conscious of or blind spots might be noticed. We also bring in external visitors to monitor, check and review different aspects of our work. Many visitors come regularly to houses for different reasons. At times, it can feel as if there are too many visitors, which can make it difficult to establish a sense of a home that does not feel institutionalized. Houses can come to lack a sense of privacy so that stepping into one does not feel like going into someone's home. This can be especially so when working with children who have little sense of boundaries and a protected space.

One of the therapeutic aims in our work with emotionally unintegrated children is to focus their relationships onto a small group of grown-ups, so they have the experience of living in a relatively contained space centered on their needs. The role of senior managers is more geared to providing support for the staff directly involved with children rather than working with children themselves. If senior managers are not directly involved in work with children, the staff who are might feel like 'it's all right for them' or 'they don't know what it's like.' However, there are also positive aspects in having a support system that is not caught up so directly in the situation or problem. There is need for a perspective that comes from being more removed. If the senior managers providing this perspective are drawn directly into work with children, it is difficult to maintain this position. It can be difficult to use people in certain ways if they are too close to the situation. Given the demands upon staff working directly with children, it is important that there is the sense of reliable support and availability in the background. If senior managers take on a role in houses the sense of external support and availability can suggest it is crisis-led, unreliable and less containing. There is also the practical difficulty for a senior manager visiting a house, should there be a complicated situation with a child perhaps requiring physical intervention. If the senior manager does not intervene, this may give a confusing message. Conversely, if she does intervene she could become embroiled in whatever follows, to the extent that her wider management role is compromised.

If a house is having trouble about safety and containment, management and authority, the role of senior manager needs careful thought if it is going to be supportive rather than undermining. It is not generally helpful for someone to come into a house during a difficult situation and take over or impose an authority that cuts across the authority of the grown-ups directly involved with children. It would only be appropriate to do so in the most extreme of situations. It is easy to undermine further the authority of grown-ups who are struggling to establish their own authority. If a senior manager goes into a house during a difficult group management situation, there can be a confusion of roles. How do the house manager and senior manager assume authority in relation to each other and working with the situation?

Usually it is supportive for those outside of the situation to focus on restoring the relationships and authority between grown-ups and children within the house. One of the potential difficulties if a senior manager intervenes within the house is that the children might perceive the grown-ups looking after them as lacking in authority and a reliance on external authority can develop. This is less likely if the intervention is instigated from within the house. It can be useful for a senior manager to go into a house to talk with a group of children about some of the straightforward aspects of reality and consequences of their behavior. For example, it is not acceptable to damage property, it causes distress and if things are damaged they must be repaired, which may cost money. Again, this is likely to be most effective when staff within the house support it. This work can also include the feelings of people outside of the house in relation to the children's behavior, the physical consequences and cost of damage. However, if the house is using the external person in place of, rather than in support of, internal authority it is not likely to improve authority within the house.

It is possible that senior managers' wish to visit houses will be connected to their anxieties related to standards of work. If this is the case, it is appropriate to check and monitor matters for these reasons, while being careful that staff and children do not themselves become anxious as a result. When anxieties about work are present there may be mixed feelings about senior managers visiting a house. Staff might feel the need for close support and some reassurance about their work as well as help to improve it, while also feeling anxious of being criticized for not working to an acceptable standard. The senior manager is likely to have similar anxieties.

Staff hours of work in relation to the therapeutic task

Cotswold staff always worked long hours because they felt it was necessary to offer the children continuity, consistency and opportunities for reliable attachment. Over time, the hours reduced from about 70 to 60 hours a week. The long hours that staff worked with children was central to the ethos, which the Community had developed, though this needed to be balanced against how this affected staff.

The high level of continuity and consistency provided for children is generally felt to be one of the main strengths in our therapeutic approach and the hours that staff work is central to this. This allows:

- the children being woken up and put to bed by the same person by having continuity throughout the day;
- staff working over from one day to the next;
- not too many staff changeovers;
- adults being at work for more time than they are away from work.

Because of staff working long hours, the size of staff teams can remain relatively small. This also enables consistency and continuity to be achieved more easily. Staff living on site also helps to give the Community a sense of being a home and more than a place where children live and adults work. The fact that staff live in the Community often seems very significant to children and it can add to their sense of security.

Working with emotional disturbance will inevitably have an impact on those involved, in particular on the staff's defense mechanisms and how they feel about themselves. It is this that can be felt to be particularly demanding and stressful for the individuals involved. The length of time exposed to this disturbance will influence the extent of the impact. One of the positive aspects of the long hours worked is that it can help carers and children to be more emotionally involved with one another, allowing strong attachments to develop. One of the behavior patterns of emotionally unintegrated children is the indiscriminate use of others, partly as a way of avoiding real and meaningful relationships. If we had more adults spending less time with children, it would be more difficult to focus relationships. It can also be difficult for adults not to use the transitory nature of work to become less emotionally involved with children. Sustaining a high level of emotional involvement would be difficult. If the level of involvement is felt to be too great or overwhelming and there is no legitimate way to withdraw, so that one's batteries may be recharged or defense mechanisms restored, then other ways of protecting oneself might develop. These could include absenting oneself from work or working but withdrawing emotionally. It is also more likely at these times that staff react to the children's disturbance in an attempt to defend themselves from it.

The wider context within which we work is likely to influence the way we feel about the work. Over the years, the hours worked by staff in residential settings such as the Community have reduced significantly. The 'Working Time Directive', with its emphasis on the 48-hour week, may have made staff even more conscious of working long hours. This external view of the 'right' way to do things has an impact whether it is entirely agreed with or not. This is similar to how cultural values interact with parenting on matters such as smacking and either support or undermine the practice.

While acknowledging the impact of working long hours with emotionally disturbed children, we need to be careful not to attribute too many difficulties to this. Some experiences will continue to be demanding, stressful and distressing regardless of the hours worked. Sometimes the wish to stay away from work can be a reaction to a difficult and upsetting situation. Some of the benefits of working long hours, such as feeling more tuned in and not constantly having to catch up with things, could be lost by working shorter hours. Shorter hours could reduce certain stresses but also create others. For example, some staff have felt the work to be more stressful following the last reduction in hours. This is partly due to feeling there is as much, if not more, to do but less time to do it in.

We need to focus on all aspects of the work and how this contributes to the way people feel at work. For instance, how is the team working together, how effective is supervision, and how is the transition to and from work managed so that there is a sense of a boundary between work and home?

The reduction of hours staff work and its impact on the therapeutic approach

A decision was made to reduce the hours to about 55 hours a week. Following this decision, there were a number of changes to practice and the way houses were managed. These changes had a significant impact on our culture and therapeutic approach. This section is particularly relevant to thinking about how we can provide continuity for children where the carers are dealing with a lot of transitions in between their time with children.

Changes to the role of focal-carer and back-up carer

With the reduction in hours it is no longer possible for these two staff to work in tandem, providing constant availability to a child throughout a week. The reduction in hours makes it more difficult to provide continuity and consistency. The back-up person who looks after a child during his carer's absence is not always the same person. Mostly two and sometimes three grown-ups share this role. Also, changes in working patterns lead to regular rearrangements of these roles. Potentially, the back-up person can have a significant role for a child as she is part of a triangular relationship with the child and his carer. These relationships can then change, develop and be used in different ways by the child as he evolves. If there are too many changes in the opportunities a child has to relate to another person other than his carer, the significance of this work could become lost or fragmented.

Another change related to the reduction in hours is an increase in staff handovers. Where there are lots of different start and finish times, it can be difficult to hold a clear pattern in mind, which might feel confusing and unpredictable. Whatever the time of the handover, we should have a clear time for saying goodbye to children. For instance, if the child is going to school in the morning and his carer is going off at 12pm it is important to say goodbye before he goes to school. Anxieties and other feelings involved in saying goodbye can contribute to the child and carer avoiding this work. It is helpful for the child that the point of separation is clear.

In these examples, the reduction in hours does not appear to benefit the children. However, if grown-ups benefit by having more time away, the quality of what is provided for children might also improve. The needs of staff and children cannot be easily separated as if they are unrelated to each other. For example, in ordinary child development, what may be the different experiences of an infant who is literally everything to his mother compared with an infant whose mother has other interests separate from him?

There is a danger in thinking of a carer's time with her child as the most positive part of his treatment and the time apart as the necessary but negative part. The child's difficulty in relation to separation can make it feel as if it is a bad thing. In such a situation, feelings of guilt might be connected to time away and a wish to somehow make up or compensate for this when together. This can reinforce the child's sense that the absence is bad for him. In reality, both the presence and absence of the carer are significant in a child's treatment. Many issues can be worked through around a carer's absence. However, for this work to be productive the absence does need to be experienced by the child as a supported space in which his feelings can be expressed and thought about.

Changes in the way houses are managed

Similar to the change in the relationship of focal-carer and back-up carer, it is no longer possible for the house manager and deputy manager to cover the house for the whole week. From day to day more staff need to become involved in the management of the house. At the same time, it has become increasingly necessary for the house manager to focus on the overall organization of the house, which is a different task than working directly with the group of children. Two to three senior staff in each house now need to be involved in managing the work with children on a day-to-day basis.

On occasions, the delegation of authority has not been clear and this has led to confusion and anxiety in the staff team. Staff are not always clear who is managing which days or how this has been decided. In some teams, the question of who is managing or who can manage seems to have become the focus for rivalry. There is a feeling that managing carries a status. This raises the question of how authority is presented and achieved in relationships with children and colleagues. The wish to manage could be a defense against the difficulty of working at these relationships. In a positive sense the taking on and sharing of responsibility can assist the growth of the team and individuals. However, when it is unclear who is actually responsible and accountable as a manager, there is a risk of no one actually feeling responsible.

The task of management is to focus on the house as a whole, thinking ahead as well as about the present, organizing and planning all the different parts, inside and outside the house. This then enables staff who are preoccupied with individual children to focus on that work without being too distracted. If there is a sense that management is unclear or lacking, it is difficult to maintain this type of preoccupation. As the manager is not the focal-carer for individual children, she can take on this task without a conflict. The manager protects the treatment relationships within the house from impingement by effective management of the house boundary.

To some extent, there is a conflict for staff who manage a day and look after individual children. Quite often children find the shift in their carer's preoccupation difficult. This can be acknowledged and worked on. One of the difficulties for an emotionally unintegrated child is to face the reality that his carer has other things to do besides looking after him. To some extent, we try to protect the children from this reality, allowing them to experience the illusion of being in the centre of things. Gradually, as this experience is internalized, the more a child will be able to acknowledge external reality and the less he will need protecting from it. If we were to work to this principle, ideally we would plan each week so that children would only be faced with their carer's other duties when appropriate in terms of their own development. Winnicott (1936) emphasizes this point well in 'Mental hygiene of the preschool child':

> Learn to bear frustration! As if we need to introduce frustrations! The inevitable frustrations of experience at toddler age, are surely enough and scarcely to be born by the most tough. (p.66)
>
> External reality changes should be made if possible when the child is not under the sway of an internal crisis. (p.70)

This last point draws attention to the importance of timing. If a staff member is going to start managing, then her work with individual children should be assessed carefully. A shift of preoccupation at a critical time can feel to the child like a rejection.

If we plan the week so that the management of each day is shared by a number of staff, we could argue that all children have to deal with the same frustrations and this is fair. If the difficulties involved can be contained, this might also be a positive experience. However, by not minimizing the number of staff who manage, it may appear as if we do not value the need for individual relationships to be protected.

Do we have enough unplanned time at work?

A reduction in hours and the demands of care standards and regulations make time seem increasingly busy and squeezed. Children need to be given a calm, secure space, where it is possible 'to be' without impingement. The sense of 'busyness' and activity can be in conflict with this.

Are we becoming increasingly busy in our work, with little time for each other informally or for creative projects? Many people feel that it is difficult to find the time to offer support and if time is found, one eye is always on the clock. When there are increasing demands on time, for example for administration, a higher proportion of time is being spent in a planned way and less in an unstructured way. Time is getting tight, leaving a sense of little room for flexibility or maneuver. One worker described the feeling as being expected to get from A to B in an unrealistic amount of time, another that she felt less in touch with staff in her team as she saw them less often. It seems that supervision, in some cases, can be used as a way of catching up with each other. Supervision should take place within the context of continuing day-to-day communication and being in touch with each other. It is a forum for focusing on specific concerns or aspects of work.

Despite the pressures, there are people in each team who can convey the sense of being available, attentive and having time. Hopefully, everyone can be in this position some of the time, but it is especially necessary for those who hold management and supervisory responsibilities. Some of this is not achieved by simply having time, but is a professional and personal quality that may need help to develop. If grown-ups do not provide that for each other, inevitably anxiety levels and a sense of insecurity will develop, which the children will notice.

Ironically, the idea of having unplanned time can create anxiety. For instance, there might be a fear it will mean spending more time with difficult children. Planned demands on time, on the other hand, can provide a safe retreat from this possibility. In reality, if grown-ups were less busy and distracted, children and grown-ups could feel more held and less anxious about getting attention.

Preserving thinking space in difficult times

When we are struggling to provide safety and containment for children, we often have less time and emotional capacity to think about our work. A knock-on effect can be that the time for thinking, such as supervision, team meetings and training, is disrupted. Paradoxically when thinking and support are most necessary there may be less time for them. The challenge is to find a balance between responding to the immediacy of situations, while keeping a sense of boundaries and not being driven to anxious reaction.

When there is a strong pull on resources to manage situations, there is often a cost to something else. Meetings and training are often eaten into. A staff member taking on extra management responsibility will have less time for other aspects of work; managers will need to spend more time organizing resources and less on other things. Alongside these matters, the general level of anxiety involved can lead to a type of culture that becomes increasingly focused on organizing, covering and planning, and less on reflecting, exploring and understanding. For example, rather than think about what a child's acting out may mean or its symbolic content, we may only see the level of seriousness or danger, and what we need to do to manage the situation. If this becomes a pattern then it is likely that we miss communication at earlier stages and a child's acting out escalates until he feels he is getting through to us in some way.

When teams are working under pressure, there is a great need to have time to think and to reflect upon the work. If this is lost, it is easy to fire-fight and be led by a sense of crisis, which may be excessively reactive and so feeds into the difficulty. A negative cycle can soon develop where things get worse rather than better. It is difficult to preserve that time to think in these circumstances. If the nature of the situation is overwhelming, feelings of self-doubt may emerge in the staff team, along with a sense of hopelessness. Anything that does not bring immediate relief to these feelings and the problems involved can seem futile. For example, if children are running off even after attempts to think about this and solve the problem, the work may seem undermined or ineffective. There could also be a growing sense of guilt felt by the adults because they have been unable to stop the behavior. Thinking and talking in supervision or consultancy might even feel like an escape from responsibility. To some extent, we should expect such feelings by the nature of the work. Our attempts to think, understand and respond are likely to be attacked.

The dilemma is crystallized where staff supervision is taking place and a child is being disruptive (this is a particular problem where education happens on site rather than away from the home). When should the supervision continue and when should it stop? If the adults continue to meet and the child's behavior gets worse, it may feel like they are being negligent and causing his behavior to deteriorate. On the other hand, if adults allow meetings and communication to be disrupted, this could feel unsafe to the child whose acting out might then escalate. Trying to be conscious of the dynamics involved and working hard at maintaining a boundary is critical. There will be times when the child must be responded to and the meeting disrupted. However, if this is done so it appears that something important has been disrupted, the message will still be that adults value communication and the spaces for this. If we get into a pattern of readily giving up these spaces, it could indicate we are letting a boundary slip. Again, if there is a high anxiety level in the team, communication can feel quite threatening. The supervisor and supervisee might feel more anxious than usual about open communication. People may feel persecuted. It is easy to withdraw into defensive noncommunication until things feel safer. In practice, things are not likely to feel safer until communication takes place.

There is also the danger in difficult periods that management and therapy become polarized and are perceived as an either-or option. As well as management predominating and possibly eroding a therapeutic culture, it can also happen the other way round. Focusing on a child's internal world and on his need for primary provision can be used as a flight from anxieties inherent in facing reality and the need for clear management. Menzies Lyth (1979) describes this clearly in her paper 'Staff support systems: task and anti-task in adolescent institutions'. She gives an example where the need to confront children's violent behavior was colluded with by staff, because of an unacknowledged fear of even greater violence from children and feelings of counter-violence in staff. The children's behavior was interpreted by staff as resulting from the staff's inadequate provision. This led to a sense of guilt and a wish to appease the children rather than confront the behavior.

Menzies Lyth points out how there is a specific danger in the caring organizations that systems, and particularly the managerial structure, become excessively infiltrated by attitudes and behavior derived from professional attitudes to therapy.

At times, effective management can also be the most therapeutic intervention. For example, physically managing a situation appropriately may be experienced by a child as feeling understood, feeling safe, having destructive feelings contained and being looked after. The management of emotionally unintegrated children has similarities with the way Winnicott (1960b) describes the mother's physical handling of her baby – it is based on an understanding of the child's needs that is fundamental to his experience and development.

It is essential that we try to preserve time for real reflection on our work with children to ensure that we are responding in a way that is based on an understanding of need. The balance of focus between internal and external reality is central to this work.

Chapter 17

Special Events

Normal childhood experiences will include special events, such as birthdays, Christmas, holidays and festivals. These events affirm one's individual and cultural identity. They can also affirm one's position in the world and specialness. They can add to one's internal store of good experiences. Traumatized children often have had negative experiences of these special events, but providing them may not be easy because of the child's mistrust and associations with previous experiences. At the same time, they provide an opportunity to work through past experiences and to provide a reaffirmation of positive experiences.

The giving and receiving of presents at Christmas

For many children and families Christmas has a major significance. Looked-after children who are away from their birth families at this time may experience this especially acutely. Those children who have no family to be with can feel especially isolated and excluded. Providing a positive experience for these children is one of the most challenging tasks involved in therapeutic care. Without awareness of the difficulties involved, each Christmas has the potential to feel like a failure which could reinforce a sense of hopelessness. Every year at the Community, an immense amount of work would go into providing an experience of Christmas and working with the matters involved. Normally this would be the most emotionally demanding time of year.

We suggested that Christmas is about giving and receiving and it was part of our task to provide children with a 'good' Christmas. This was associated with a fun time, enjoying things together, a magical time, with excitement and anticipation. As well as this, we needed to take account of whatever an individual child actually feels about Christmas. This is likely to include matters related to previous Christmases, feelings related to general matters that can surface in a powerful way at Christmas and feelings about the child's present situation. Christmas can become a focus for present and past relationships and is traditionally a family time. The Christmas we provide is likely to become a focus for the child to express feelings about these matters, while offering opportunity for working through some of them. The staff will also have their own feelings about Christmas and this will contribute to the emotional climate. Thus being aware of how one feels oneself helps to prevent what is felt being acted out or attributed to the child in an unhelpful way.

Giving and receiving presents can be difficult for the following reasons:

- disappointment and not getting what you hope for;
- worrying about what to get, getting it wrong and being rejected;
- a sense of being misunderstood and let down (how could you get me that!);
- an anxiety of being expected to please the giver by being excited and thankful;
- the anxiety of being controller or controlled (now you owe me one or how can I ever thank you?);
- rivalry over who got what;
- anticlimax.

It is important that the carer also likes the gift she is giving. It could represent something enjoyed and shared between two people in a relationship. From this point of view, we wondered whether giving children presents from the house as a whole, rather than those given by individuals, might detract from this experience.

The idea of advent boxes with a small gift for each morning building up to Christmas was also mentioned. Some years, children have made their own boxes and each morning an adult puts in a small gift in each child's box. It was suggested this can create a 'Christmassy' feel and a sense of anticipation. It can also help give the children something that feels manageable to focus on each day rather than just wait for Christmas Day. We were unsure whether it is better to do this or put the emphasis on waiting and work with the feelings involved in that.

One year the experience of Christmas was very positive and, in part, this seemed connected to the decision made by the team to buy each adult a present, as well as the children. This seemed more natural and less contrived than the adults just giving the children presents and watching them opening them. During the period before Christmas children were excited and some of them made presents for adults. This can be very significant for a child's development and it is important that adults are receptive to a child's wish to give (see Winnicott 1963 on the importance of the infant being able to 'contribute' towards the mother).

If adults are giving each other a gift, this should be secondary to the children receiving their presents. The adults should not distract each other or the children too much because they are giving an opportunity for a child to notice something if he is ready or wants to. A child may be relieved to see adults giving to each other. This could reflect a continuing sense of care and communication between adults that is restorative and resilient. At the same time, a child might not be able to think about this and should not have it imposed upon him.

Birthdays

Like Christmas, birthdays can arouse powerful emotions related to past experiences, relationships and one's present circumstances. Birthdays can evoke strong feelings about oneself and relationships with others. This can be both a hopeful time of anticipation and excitement as well as anxiety. For traumatized and deprived children the anxiety involved can overwhelm positive aspects associated with their birthday.

It is important to think about what the child might like for his birthday presents, as well as making it a special type of experience. Some children go out with their carer for a birthday meal or they do something else the child asks to do. We make a cake for the child, designed in a way special to him, and give it to him in the group. Some children like to be given their presents in the morning in their room, others are happy to have them in the group. Each child is thought about in terms of what his birthday means to him, how we help him with his feelings and provide him with a 'good' experience, and how his family and others are involved.

Whatever a child's previous experiences and anxieties he has about his birthday – such as that he does not deserve to have a good one – we should give him the message that his birthday is a special day. We can try to do things in the way he would realistically like. If he wants to reject the whole thing, we should continue to provide him with a birthday, but also respect his feelings and not be too pushy.

It is helpful to establish some group expectations of birthdays as well as what it can mean for individuals. By being involved to some extent with each birthday, children can get a sense of what kind of birthday to expect and to see some consistency and reliability. If there was not some consistency it is likely that the uncertainty of what to expect, the possibility of being let down and other anxieties would become too overwhelming.

Wherever possible we should involve a child's parents by discussing and planning the birthday with them, and arranging any contact between them and their child.

Group holidays

Many residential homes arrange for children to go on a group holiday at least once a year. This is a significant and demanding time. Traumatized and deprived children, who become reliant on the safety of where they are, including the daily routines and familiarity, can find the changes and uncertainties in going away unsettling and it can make them anxious, as it can adults, but it can also be a rewarding time and an opportunity for growth.

There are clearly anxieties involved for children and adults in going away on holiday and being in a different situation together. If these anxieties can be contained, the potentially difficult experience can develop into a good one. This can be of great benefit in a child's treatment. He might sense that his difficulties are not so overwhelming that the holiday is impossible and that he can be contained or held away from the home as well as in it. The achievement of managing a new experience, trying out new things and generally having a good time can build self-confidence and be emotionally stored as a positive experience and memory.

Holidays are intense situations. There may be little privacy and adults' normal break away from work will be lost. Some of this anxiety is specifically focused on sleeping arrangements. For example, who sleeps in the dormitory with the boys and should women be expected to? Some women feel very uncomfortable about this from a sexual point of view. It is important to listen to the children's and grown-ups' anxieties when deciding about this.

The daily routines and structures will obviously be different. Anchor points in the daily routine do not exist in the same way. However, mealtimes can still provide an anchor point. Picnic lunches for trips out can often have the same effect. Different routines or traditions may evolve (Dockar-Drysdale 1990j). She describes one occasion when the drawing of pictures about the holiday became an enjoyable part of each day for children and adults. At supper time, great delight was taken in this, while a story was read and supper served. Adaptations and bedtime visits that children have when in the home do not usually go on the same way during holidays. It is helpful to talk with children about these changes a week or two before the holiday and to think about how they might affect each child. It is also important to talk and think about what children would like to take on holiday with them. Personal possessions and objects such as blanket, teddy or toy can help to give the child a sense of familiarity and security.

When we are away on holiday we may worry how will children behave in public, how will we react and how will members of the public react? While having certain expectations of children, we should take responsibility and not put them in situations that would be too difficult for them to deal with.

Communication between the staff team can be difficult during the holiday as there is not always much space or time. Though it can be difficult for adults to talk to each other as much as they would wish and find time for each other, it is important that this should be the aim: to try to ensure that the whole team feels held. Making a point of talking with each other at the end of the day will help.

There are other matters too, that are raised by holidays and these include being more exposed to each other's personal habits, how adults might have some time away during the week, the increased anxiety about safety and the possibility of accidents.

Chapter 18

Other Questions, Other Possibilities

Working with children's parents

Many children in residential care have regular contact with their birth family and parents. Some of these children are accommodated rather than on care orders – they are voluntarily in care and their parents are able to remove them. The best care is that which tries to work in partnership with parents. This work can be challenging and difficult for all involved and can, at times, feel impossible.

It can sometimes be the case that work with the parents of some children can be so difficult that some staff working directly with children feel a conflict between the two. For example, a phone call from a parent can become extremely demanding and might go on for quite a while – this can make staff feel as if they are being taken away from the group of children, as well as causing problems in working with the child of the parents concerned. When a parent is conveying a strong sense of mistrust and is making an attack on the adult concerned, she may feel that her work is being undermined. This can cause staff to react against the child as well as the parents. It is important to acknowledge that these dynamics might also mirror how the parents are experiencing or perceiving the staff's relationship with them.

A model derived from psychotherapy with children is that the therapist working with the child is a different person to the one working with the parents. This can help to separate what is involved and helps to protect the therapist-child relationship from impingement (Dockar-Drysdale 1960b). At the Community, it has seemed as if we have had this degree of protection and there has come a time when carers became more involved in the work with parents. However, the Community has always worked with children's parents and those working most closely with children have been central to this (see Dockar-Drysdale 1969).

Before the Children Act 1989 parents of children in care were often perceived and treated very negatively, and did not receive much support or encouragement to be involved with their children. Following the Act, the emphasis was more towards keeping a child with his own family wherever possible and involving the parents in partnership in looking after their children. Partly because of these changes, parents are more involved and empowered in the care of their children. The Act also supported the right of access the child has to his parents. Therefore, children are entitled to make phone calls without unnecessary restriction.

Where there is a clear sense of partnership between all of those involved in a child's care and education, the overall benefits to his treatment are clear. However, when there are conflicts in this partnership, this is not so. The staff member could feel that she does not have the authority to make decisions about the child's care and may feel greatly undermined. Similarly the parents might feel further undermined in their parental relationship and under attack as parents. Feelings of envy can be connected to this, for instance, envy of the parent-child relationship, the carer-child relationship, or of the care and provision the child is receiving.

Partly because of the reasons outlined above, staff teams might feel particularly vulnerable to attack and the sense that residential staff feel protected may be lost. An example which may contribute to staff feeling vulnerable was when at the Community a new telephone system allowed parents to phone directly to houses. The previous system meant that calls were received by a central switchboard and then put through to houses. This allowed staff in houses to have a few seconds to think how to respond most appropriately, rather than, without warning, suddenly having a parent on the phone. It has never been the policy to stop access (unless prohibited) and houses needing support can redirect their calls to the switchboard or senior manager.

Difficult and complex work with parents can sometimes make staff feel they lack the necessary skills to do the work. Is residential child care just about the treatment of children or is it also about working with parents? Are we trained for one and not the other? Child care social work today is very much about working in partnership with parents. When staff experience emotions such as inadequacy and vulnerability, this may be transference to us of intolerable feelings experienced by the parents. Rather than avoid these feelings we need to develop the support structures that are necessary to contain and make sense of them. These feelings may be uncomfortable, but being more distant from a parent may also be difficult. The sense of not knowing what a child and his parents are talking about will be noticed by the child and can soon lead to complicated splits. If communication is mainly between the parents and senior managers, this can undermine staff teams.

Work with parents can involve many different things: sharing information; thinking together about a child; planning and decision making; supporting the parents to help them have a positive experience with their child (this might also involve providing for the parents); listening; and being available. As the amount of work in these areas has been increasing, we need to be more specific in the ways we respond. For instance, evenings may not be the best time for doing difficult work with parents, in which case we can explain why and then be firm about it. A reliable time during the day could be offered.

In addition, we need to decide which work should be done by the house and which by senior staff outside of the house. These matters are not always straightforward. What can start as a routine piece of work between worker and parents can become complicated due to underlying tensions.

Bedwetting and soiling

Bedwetting and soiling are common symptoms in traumatized children. The combination of possible physical, emotional and medical matters makes this complex and requires a thoughtful and informed response.

When a child wets his bed, we generally respond by changing his sheets for him, clean his bed and care for him by preparing his bath. Grown-ups will have different feelings about this at different times. They may enjoy making up a child's bed again and caring for him in this way; they may change his bed in a mechanical way, almost shutting out thoughts about bedwetting; they may be disgusted. Quite often the issue is responded to without saying much to the child about it, sometimes it is talked about in an exploratory way and at times a more direct approach is adopted. For example, the child is praised if he is dry, expected to help in changing his bed and getting his bath, and is helped to moderate drinks taken late at night.

Both emotionally unintegrated and integrated children might wet, though it is predominately unintegrated children who do so. The bedwetting tends to stop as the children evolve emotionally. With some children, it feels as though they could stop but choose to carry on. It may feel aggressive and evoke strong feelings in the carers.

There are a number of different areas to consider in trying to understand why different children wet or soil. Sometimes there are physical or medical reasons why they do so. This needs checking. The bedwetting could be part of a general regression. The child may be returning to a point where he needs concrete experiences of provision or feeling contained. In this sense, the child's body can be seen as a metaphor for a container – in the same way he is unable to contain feelings in his mind, his body is unable to contain his own urine and feces.

The child's wetting or soiling could be seen as, literally, giving his carer something to look after and contain. This means the carer's response to the wetting and the relationship it happens within is of central importance. As well as responding to the actual bedwetting in a caring way, we should also ask ourselves what issues might be connected with it. For example, is the child scared at night, anxious about something, or feeling angry? In a similar way, bedwetting may feel like a concrete way of getting rid of bad feelings, with the urine representing bad feelings. There could be some hostility towards the child's carer in this. It is difficult for the child to experience and contain aggressive feelings towards someone about whom he also cares. Wetting or soiling himself can be a way of managing these feelings that is less threatening than, for example, being physically violent.

Wetting and soiling are often associated with uncontrollable fear or laughter. Both are extremes of different feelings and are overwhelming or too much to contain and hold onto. The children may have little capacity to contain powerful feelings such as fear. As a child's capacity to contain feelings develops, he may begin to wet and soil less often. If the wetting carries on beyond a point that seems related to the child's emotional development, there might be other concerns. These could involve physical or sexual abuse, or represent a kind of behavior that needs managing by changing our expectations of the child. There might be an element of training or helping the child to take some responsibility for his bedwetting.

We should think about what we feel about bedwetting and soiling and not respond to the child in a way that makes him feel he is bad or disgusting – he will already have some of these anxieties. For example, we should try to enable children to enjoy baths or showers after bedwetting or soiling. Baths and showers can seem punitive to the child. It is also important that children who wet have baths at other times, so that bathing is not always associated with wetting.

Children's clothing and appearance

Like all of us, a child's appearance will reflect how he feels about himself. Some children, who have low self-esteem, will ensure that however much effort is put into caring for them, they quickly look disheveled and uncared for. In some cases, this is connected to a lack of value for oneself and chaotic behavior. In others, it is a more conscious attempt to spoil and destroy their clothing and appearance. The opposite can also occur – a child can take great care and pride in his appearance as a defensive facade to hide the emptiness he feels inside. In some cases, possibly in work with a child who has developed a pseudomaturity as a way of coping, it can be a healthy development that the child takes less care of himself and allows a grown-up to take care of him. It can be important to be messy and to have this cared for, as this allows him to have an experience he needs.

But how does a child's appearance reflect our attitude towards him? For example, do we get into the role of being the depriving, depressed or overwhelmed carer and give up on bothering what he looks like or making sure he is dressed appropriately for the weather? Do we try to get away from the difficulty of thinking about a child and his feelings by becoming too concerned with how he looks? It is positive to convey the message to children that we care about how they look as part of our general care for them.

Putting a child in new or well-kept clothes will not make him a different person. However, it can be one of the ways a grown-up shows care, which he can gradually understand and take in. In this sense, being in cared-for clothes can feel different from being in ones that are tatty or torn. If a child does perceive this as care, it is also likely he will test the reliability of it by spoiling his clothes to see if the grown-up will persist or give up.

When it comes to clothes, there can be a difficulty for children whose families are unable to provide the quality of care and clothing that we provide. In some cases, on returning home a child's new clothing has been shared out among other members of his family. In others, a child's siblings have felt envious of him and his parents have had feelings about the perceived difference between the home's provision and theirs. These feelings can also be difficult for the child to manage. He might feel guilty that the rest of his family does not have the same as him. He could also feel disloyal to his family as if he is rejecting their care in favor of the home's. Even where there is little actual contact between a child and his family, he may have an internal image of his parents to which he feels loyal and protective. Clothing can be a concrete representation of provision in general and be the focus for other feelings related to this. A child may manage this type of difficulty by constantly destroying and spoiling his clothing. The child could appear to be rejecting our care through this behavior, though remain open to forms of primary provision that are less visible, for example, enjoying bedtime stories.

While all of a child's clothes should be of a reasonable standard, he should have some clothes for 'best' as well as clothes for playing. Some children like dressing up and looking smart, whether to go round town or to a special event. Others need much help in dressing appropriately. Some children like to wear their best clothes all of the time. This is an area where a child and grown-up need to strike a balance. For emotionally integrated children, arguments about what can or cannot or should be worn are often related to individuality and how this is negotiated. The more unintegrated children will need a grown-up to be responsible for looking after and organizing their clothes for them. The grown-up can present the child with a small choice of clothes he would like to wear. This also helps a child develop a sense of his own identity.

Similarly with buying of clothes, unintegrated children can be encouraged to shop and help choose their own clothes, though a grown-up will be responsible for budgeting. As well as thinking about the individual child, the grown-up will also need to think what is appropriate for the group as a whole. Certain types of clothing are unsuitable because of the associations connected with them. There may also be children who want to wear the same style of clothes as each other, and the underlying reasons for this will need assessing. Some unintegrated children prefer a grown-up to take complete responsibility for choosing and buying their clothes. As children become more integrated or mature, they will need to make more of their own choices, within a realistic budget.

Children buying their own teddy bears

At the Community many children had their own teddies which they had either brought with them or asked for once they were there. In many cases, the teddies were very special to the children, perhaps being the only thing they had left from their mother or a special teddy given to them by their carer. The teddies tended to be used to symbolically represent an important relationship or as an extension of the child's identity. In this case, the child would often use the teddy in play and communicate through the teddy. At one time a number of children had been buying their own teddies and some of them were doing this in a teasing and aggressive way towards other children. In particular, it seemed to arise when one child was envious of anything 'special' a carer would provide for another child. While this is true of teddies, the same can apply to any kind of special provision made to a child and the reactions of other children to it.

Teddies are a significant part of provision in the Community. Children often ask for a 'special teddy' from their focal-carer. This teddy then becomes something special between the child and adult and to some extent signifies their relationship. The teddy could at times become a 'self-object', representing parts of the child or a 'transitional object' (Winnicott 1951), representing something between the child and adult.

There are different ways of considering the teddy issue. For example, allowing children to buy their own teddies could undermine their 'specialness'. This could be an attack on provision. A child who has a 'special' teddy provided for him might buy another as a way of rejecting the provision. Children may buy teddies as a way of enviously attacking 'special' provision made to another child – 'Look what I've got!' There could be an aspect of self-provision – 'I don't need anyone to give me anything – I can get it myself.'

Another point of view is to focus on the difference between something that is special and something that is not. If we do that rather than control what children buy, children who have something special might realize that it cannot be spoilt that easily. Children buying their own teddies may also realize they cannot create something 'special' on their own.

Other points to consider are:

- The child might not be concerned with teddies in any particular way and could just want to buy a teddy.
- He could need to experience providing things for himself and see what it is like.
- Buying teddies may be better than buying other things we do not let children buy.
- Buying a teddy could be a way of symbolically rejecting provision, rather than attacking it more directly.
- What do we think and feel about teddies, for example, are they babyish? Our own feelings will affect the children's attitude.

In practice, we should be able to tell what the issues are by looking at the way a child uses his teddy and what it means to him. If our provision is generally under attack, it is not easy to tolerate children undermining it further. The feelings stirred up are difficult to contain. A child with a fragile sense of good experiences might easily feel his 'special thing' has been spoilt, if other children are allowed to go and buy something his carer has just given to him. Similarly, it is easy for adults to feel whatever they provide is worthless. During such a period or situation, it can be appropriate to protect provision by making a clear rule that children do not buy teddies. Good support and teamwork will help to contain these feelings.

Tickling and play fighting

Tickling and play fighting are common between children and adults. Both can be fun and enjoyed by adults and children alike. However, this is not always the case for traumatized children who may have been physically and sexually abused, as it can raise complicated and confusing feelings about power and boundaries.

Tickling and play fighting are both inappropriate for adults to do to or with children. There are a number of reasons for this. Tickling can create a situation where one person is totally out of control, helpless at the hands of someone else. It establishes a relationship based on power. It can also be teasing. The children we work with have not had their bodies and personal boundaries respected. Therefore, they have little sense of a boundary and cannot be expected to say 'yes' or 'no' to tickling. Tickling and play fighting are both quite invasive and may echo any experiences of abuse the child has had. To help children establish the idea that their bodies do belong to them, we need to create a sense of personal boundaries that is very clear.

Tickling and play fighting can stir up sexual and aggressive feelings that are not helpful in an environment where these feelings are barely contained. As tickling and play fighting are meant to be 'just fun', it can be hard to acknowledge any difficulties that arise. These feelings might then come out somewhere else. Tickling and play fighting can be confusing to a child who has been hurt physically or emotionally by someone who also loved him. The distinction between being cared for and being hurt is blurred. We need to give a clear message that being cared for does not mean being hurt. It is also confusing in other ways. Where is the line between play and fighting? Who can do it to whom – adult to child, child to adult, and is there any difference when one is male and one is female?

If a child tickles or attempts to play fight, we should respond in a way that does not encourage it to continue, but also does not leave the child feeling rejected. It might be difficult for the child to know how to make contact. He could also be testing to see if the adult will become involved inappropriately. It is helpful to be open to different physical approaches from a child, as it tells us something significant about him, but not necessarily to join in with it. At times, it will be necessary to say 'no' clearly to him. By making our own boundaries clear, we will also help him begin to get a sense of his own.

Peer group relationships for children

Relationships between emotionally traumatized children who are living together have to be monitored closely due to the risks involved. However, if this is too restrictive, children are denied the opportunity of forming relationships and enjoying and learning from them. We can be too anxious about children wanting to be together and this has to be balanced against an overly permissive approach, which does not provide enough protection.

Do we pay enough attention to the positive aspects of relationships between children as part of the therapeutic environment? In 'normal' child development, relationships between brothers and sisters and children the same age are often acknowledged as making a significant contribution to an evolving personality. Bruno Bettleheim (1970) in his study of Kibbutz children described his own surprise at realizing the extent to which infants as young as two were able to contribute towards each other in a positive way, providing companionship, care and even security for each other.

Clearly, the children we work with have suffered great deprivation of primary provision and have a confused sense of relationships. Our emphasis with emotionally unintegrated children is to meet a child's need for primary provision, mainly through establishing a dependant attachment with his carer. With emotionally integrated children, there is more emphasis on the relationships between everyone in the group and the experience of this is central to the therapeutic approach.

Although the individual relationship between carer and child is central to our work, children do spend a lot of time together in groups and work with children takes place in groups. The positive contribution a child can make to the group as well as to individual people plays an integral part in his development. We tend to view this mostly in terms of reparation, communication and showing empathy. These qualities, while not necessarily implying attachments between children, show how children who are emotionally held can begin to relate positively to others.

Do we allow room for the possibility of friendship between children? It is usual for small children to have a best friend though these relationships are often transient. On the other hand, friendships from infancy and early school years may go into adulthood. The relationships between children are often important and some continue after leaving residential care. This sometimes happens between the younger as well as the older children. There are examples where contact has continued for years and developed into a friendship, giving both children some companionship on leaving the home as young adults. Other children have talked of their home being like a family. Some children leave and want to renew contact with children who were with them. A residential home might be the place where the largest period is spent during their entire childhood. Unlike a family, the children may never see or hear from each other once they have left. This can be a great loss and leave a gap in the child's history.

An anxiety is the potentially destructive relationship between children with the possibility of bullying, sexual abuse and dangerous acting out.

Another concern is that the children are mistrustful of adults and allowing any dependence to develop, and could use relationships with other children as a form of self-provision. For these reasons, it is necessary for us to manage the environment so that each child is able to develop the kind of relationships he needs with his carers. However, we need to focus on the child's emerging personality and be careful not to give children too many negative messages about their emotional difficulties.

While it is not possible for an emotionally unintegrated child to have a relationship with a clear sense of boundaries, we can help manage difficulties for him so that he can experience positive relationships with others. But by being anxious about relationships between children, we might respond to any notion that a child has of friendship in a dismissive way. This could feel crushing to him, as if any relationship between him and another child can only be negative. Paradoxically, this could actually cause children to perceive all their relationships with each other as 'bad', sexual, secretive and thus could lead them to develop them in this way.

Bettleheim (1974) has argued that it is preferable for children to sleep in dormitories with some sort of boundary to mark their own personal space. He found that it was not helpful for children who might feel insecure and anxious at night to be put in a room on their own. It has often been the case on group holidays that once initial excitement has been worked through, children have enjoyed the experience of sleeping in close proximity to others, as long as adults provide appropriate support. Another example at the Community was a group sleeping together in the lounge to provide a sense of security for each other during a thunderstorm.

What has been said in this section reminds us again how complex the issues can be but we need to remember, too, that the anxieties about child protection can preoccupy us so that we lose sight of all other perspectives and needs. We may not have much empathy for a child's wish to be with another child.

The possible implications of lockable cupboards or boxes for children

Historically the Community had moved away from the notion that things should be locked up. The only locked room in the house would be the office with children's files, medicine and petty cash. It was felt that locks were associated with the culture of the Approved School and institutional care. The idea that children should be provided with a lockable box or cupboard for their personal belongings was recommended through the inspection process.

The idea of introducing a locked box for each child to keep in their bedrooms so that possessions can be kept safe raises a number of anxieties. What is hidden in the boxes? What anxieties does the group have about this?

From a therapeutic point of view, there are potential difficulties. For example, the child may wonder why we are suggesting that he locks things away and keeps them hidden. The idea of a lockable box for each child feels too concrete. Containment needs to come from within, not be imposed from outside. We help children develop a sense of separation and personal space. We try to establish this in our culture and defend it. For instance, if a child says, 'don't look in my drawer', we can respect his request, helping him develop a sense of personal boundaries, whereas a locked box implies mistrust and no choice. Locked boxes feel like a move away from containment, privacy and safety to exclusion and being locked out. A child needs to find his own way in how and what he lets or keeps in or out. Imposing a locked box does not help him in differentiating his emerging self.

In this context there is no therapeutic justification for giving children a lockable box or cupboard. If it has to happen, can it be done in a more personal and less exclusive way? This could be by the carer and child making a box together and both having a key.

References

Bettleheim, B. (1970) *The Children of the Dream.* New York: Avon Books.

Bettleheim, B. (1974) *A Home for the Heart.* London: Thames and Hudson.

Bettleheim, B. (1990) *Recollections and Reflections.* London: Thames and Hudson.

Bion, W. R. (1962) *Learning from Experience.* London: Karnac Books/Heinemann.

Burn, M. (1956) *Mr. Lyward's Answer.* Hamish Hamilton Ltd.

Copley, B. and Forryan, B. (1987) *Therapeutic Work with Children and Young People.* London: Cassel. (1997)

Department of Health (1991) *The Children Act 1989 Guidance and Regulations: Volume 4 Residential Care.* London: The Stationery Office.

Department of Health/Department of Education and Employment (2000) *Guidance on the Education of Children and Young People in Public Care.* London: The Stationery Office.

Dockar-Drysdale, B. (1953) 'Some aspects of damage and restitution.' In B. Dockar-Drysdale (1993a).

Dockar-Drysdale, B. (1958) 'Residential treatment of "frozen" children.' In B. Dockar-Drysdale (1993a).

Dockar-Drysdale, B. (1960a) 'The outsider and the insider in a therapeutic school.' In B. Dockar-Drysdale (1993a).

Dockar-Drysdale, B. (1960b) 'Contact, impact and impingement.' In B. Dockar-Drysdale (1990a).

Dockar-Drysdale, B. (1961) 'The problem of making adaptation to the needs of the individual child in a group.' In B. Dockar-Drysdale (1990a).

Dockar-Drysdale, B. (1963a) 'The process of symbolisation observed among emotionally deprived children in a therapeutic school.' In B. Dockar-Drysdale (1990a).

Dockar-Drysdale, B. (1963b) 'The possibility of regression in a structured environment.' In B. Dockar-Drysdale (1993a).

Dockar-Drysdale, B. (1966) 'The provision of primary experience in a therapeutic school.' In B. Dockar-Drysdale (1993a).

Dockar-Drysdale, B. (1969) 'Emotionally deprived parents.' In B. Dockar-Drysdale (1993a).

Dockar-Drysdale, B. (1970a) 'Need assessment – 1, Finding a basis.' In B. Dockar-Drysdale (1993a).

Dockar-Drysdale, B. (1970b) 'Need assessment – 2, Making an assessment.' In B. Dockar-Drysdale (1993a).

Dockar-Drysdale, B. (1971) 'The management of violence in disturbed children.' In B. Dockar-Drysdale (1993a).

Dockar-Drysdale, B. (1980) 'Collusive anxiety in the residential treatment of disturbed adolescents.' In B. Dockar-Drysdale (1990a).

Dockar-Drysdale, B. (1987) 'Therapy and the first year of life.' In B. Dockar-Drysdale (1990a).
Dockar-Drysdale, B. (1990a) *The Provision of Primary Experience: Winnicottian Work with Children and Adolescents.* London: Free Association Books.
Dockar-Drysdale, B. (1990b) 'Need assessments and context profiles.' In B. Dockar-Drysdale (1990a).
Dockar-Drysdale, B. (1990c) 'About integration.' In B. Dockar-Drysdale (1990a).
Dockar-Drysdale, B. (1990d) 'Staff consultation in an evolving care system.' In B. Dockar-Drysdale (1990a).
Dockar-Drysdale, B. (1990e) 'Therapy and the first year of life.' In B. Dockar-Drysdale (1990a).
Dockar-Drysdale, B. (1990f) 'Collusive anxiety in the residential treatment of disturbed adolescents.' In B. Dockar-Drysdale (1990a).
Dockar-Drysdale, B. (1990g) 'Holding.' In B. Dockar-Drysdale (1990a).
Dockar-Drysdale, B. (1990h) 'Panic.' In B. Dockar-Drysdale (1990a).
Dockar-Drysdale, B. (1990i) 'The management of violence.' In B. Dockar-Drysdale (1990a).
Dockar-Drysdale, B. (1990j) 'Id sublimation.' In B. Dockar-Drysdale (1990a).
Dockar-Drysdale, B. (1993a) *Therapy and Consultation in Child Care.* London: Free Association Books.
Dockar-Drysdale, B. (1993b) 'Therapy in child care.' In B. Dockar-Drysdale (1993a).
Fonagy, P. (2001) *Attachment Theory and Psychoanalysis.* New York: Other Press.
Fraiberg, S. (ed) (1980) 'Ghosts in the nursery.' In *Clinical Studies in Infant Mental Health: The First Year of Life.* London: Tavistock.
Hancock, P., Simmons, S. and Whitwell, J. (1990) 'The importance of food in relation to the treatment of deprived and disturbed children in care.' In *International Journal of Therapeutic Communities 11*, 2, 103–111.
Kennedy, R., Heymans, A. and Tischler, L. (1987) *The Family as In-Patient.* London: Free Association Books.
Menzies Lyth, I. (1979) 'Staff support systems: task and anti-task in adolescent institutions.' In I. Menzies Lyth (1988).
Menzies Lyth, I. (1985) 'The development of the self in children in institutions.' In I. Menzies Lyth (1988).
Menzies Lyth, I. (1988) *Containing Anxiety in Institutions: Selected Essays Vol 1.* London: Free Association Books.
Miller, E.J. (1993) The Healthy Organisation. *Creating a Holding Environment: Conditions for Psychological Security.* London: The Tavistock Institute.
Oxford Pocket Dictionary (1992). New York: Oxford University Press.
Redl, F. (1966) *When We Deal with Children.* New York: Free Press.
Rollinson, R. (2003) 'Leadership in a therapeutic environment: What a long, strange trip it is.' In A. Ward, K. Kasinski, J. Pooley and A. Worthington (eds) *Therapeutic Communities for Children and Young People.* London and New York: Jessica Kingsley Publishers.
Rose, M. (1987) 'The function of food in residential treatment.' In *Journal of Adolescence 10*, 149–162.
Rose, M. (1990) *Healing Hurt Minds: The Peper Harow Experience.* London: Tavistock/Routledge.

Shapiro, E.R. and Carr, A.W. (1991) *Lost in Familiar Places.* New Haven and London: Yale University Press.
Ward, A. (1998) 'Helping together.' In A. Ward and L. McMahon (eds) *Intuition Is Not Enough.* London and New York: Routledge.
Winnicott, D.W. (1936) 'Mental hygiene of the preschool child.' In D.W. Winnicott (1996).
Winnicott, D.W. (1947) 'Hate in the counter-transference.' In D.W. Winnicott (1975).
Winnicott, D.W. (1949) 'Birth memories, birth trauma and anxiety.' In D.W. Winnicott (2002).
Winnicott, D.W. (1951) 'Transitional objects and phenomena.' In D.W. Winnicott (2002).
Winnicott, D.W. (1956a) 'Primary maternal preoccupation.' In D.W. Winnicott (1975).
Winnicott, D.W. (1956b) 'The antisocial tendency.' D.W. Winnicott (2002).
Winnicott, D.W. (1960a) 'Ego distortion in terms of true and false self.' In D.W. Winnicott (1990).
Winnicott, D.W. (1960b) 'The theory of the parent-infant relationship'.In D.W. Winnicott (1990).
Winnicott, D.W. (1962) 'Ego integration in child development.' In D.W. Winnicott (1990).
Winnicott, D.W. (1963) 'The development of the capacity for concern.' In D.W. Winnicott (1990).
Winnicott, D.W. (1964) 'The world in small doses.' In *The Child, the Family, and the Outside World.* Hammondsworth: Penguin Books.
Winnicott, D.W. (1971) *Playing and Reality.* London: Tavistock.
Winnicott, D.W. (1975) *Through Paediatrics to Psychoanalysis* London: Hogarth Press and Institute of Psychoanalysis.
Winnicott, D.W. (1986) *Home Is Where we Start From.* Harmondsworth: Penguin Books.
Winnicott, D.W. (1990) *The Maturational Process and the Facilitating Environment.* London and New York: Karnac Books.
Winnicott, D.W. (1996) *Thinking about Children.* London and New York: Karnac Books.
Winnicott, D.W. (2002) *Through Paediatrics to Psychoanalysis.* London: Karnac Books.

Subject Index

Author Index

Printed in Dunstable, United Kingdom

91336272R00127